The Last to Fall

"Authors Jim Rada and Richard Fulton have done an outstanding job of researching and chronicling this little-known story of those Marines in 1922, marking it as a significant moment in Marine Corps history."

- *GySgt. Thomas Williams*
Executive Director
U.S. Marine Corps Historical Company

"Original, unique, profusely illustrated throughout, exceptionally well researched, informed, informative, and a bit iconoclastic, "The Last to Fall: The 1922 March, Battles, & Deaths of U.S. Marines at Gettysburg" will prove to be of enormous interest to military buffs and historians."

- *Small Press Bookwatch*

Saving Shallmar

"But Saving Shallmar's Christmas story is a tale of compassion and charity, and the will to help fellow human beings not only survive, but also be ready to spring into action when a new opportunity presents itself. Bittersweet yet heartwarming, Saving Shallmar is a wonderful Christmas season story for readers of all ages and backgrounds, highly recommended."

- *Small Press Bookwatch*

Battlefield Angels

"Rada describes women religious who selflessly performed life-saving work in often miserable conditions and thereby gained the admiration and respect of countless contemporaries. In so doing, Rada offers an appealing narrative and an entry point into the wealth of sources kept by the sisters."

- *Catholic News Service*

Between Rail and River
"The book is an enjoyable, clean family read, with characters young and old for a broad-based appeal to both teens and adults. Between Rail and River also provides a unique, regional appeal, as it teaches about a particular group of people, ordinary working 'canawlers' in a story that goes beyond the usual coverage of life during the Civil War."
- Historical Fiction Review

Canawlers
"A powerful, thoughtful and fascinating historical novel, Canawlers documents author James Rada, Jr. as a writer of considerable and deftly expressed storytelling talent."
- *Midwest Book Review*

"James Rada, of Cumberland, has written a historical novel for high-schoolers and adults, which relates the adventures, hardships and ultimate tragedy of a family of boaters on the C&O Canal. ... The tale moves quickly and should hold the attention of readers looking for an imaginative adventure set on the canal at a critical time in history."
- *Along the Towpath*

October Mourning
"This is a very good, and very easy to read, novel about a famous, yet unknown, bit of 20th Century American history. While reading this book, in your mind, replace all mentions of 'Spanish Flu' with 'bird flu.' Hmmm."
- *Reviewer's Bookwatch*

SECRETS OF
GARRETT COUNTY

Little-Known Stories & Hidden History
of Maryland's Westernmost County

Other books by James Rada, Jr.

Non-Fiction
- Battlefield Angels: The Daughters of Charity Work as Civil War Nurses
- Beyond the Battlefield: Stories from Gettysburg's Rich History
- Echoes of War Drums: The Civil War in Mountain Maryland
- The Last to Fall: The 1922 March, Battles & Deaths of U.S. Marines at Gettysburg
- Looking Back: True Stories of Mountain Maryland
- Looking Back II: More True Stories of Mountain Maryland
- No North, No South: The Grand Reunion at the 50th Anniversary of the Battle of Gettysburg
- Saving Shallmar: Christmas Spirit in a Coal Town

Fiction
- Between Rail and River
- Canawlers
- Lock Ready
- October Mourning
- The Rain Man

SECRETS OF GARRETT COUNTY

Little-Known Stories & Hidden History
of Maryland's Westernmost County

by
James Rada, Jr.

LEGACY
PUBLISHING

A division of AIM Publishing Group

SECRETS OF GARRETT COUNTY: LITTLE-KNOWN STORIES
AND HIDDEN HISTORY OF MARYLAND'S WESTERNMOST
COUNTY

Published by Legacy Publishing, a division of AIM Publishing Group.
Gettysburg, Pennsylvania.
First printing: February 2017.

ISBN 978-0-9985542-1-1

This is a collection primarily of articles that have previously appeared in
*The Oakland Republican, The Glades Star, the Cumberland Times-News,
Maryland Life,* and *Saving Shallmar: Christmas Spirit in a Coal Town.* In
some cases where additional information is available the stories have
been updated.

Cover design by Grace Eyler.

LEGACY
PUBLISHING

315 Oak Lane • Gettysburg, Pennsylvania 17325

To Robin Bosley,
My favorite sister even if she is my only sister.

CONTENTS

CRIME AND PUNISHMENT

Who Killed Frank Olson?

T wo bottles of Cointreau sat on the table in front of Frank Olson. Both were open. Both were the same. He reached out for one of the bottles to pour himself an after-dinner drink. He was relaxing in a cabin with other men who had been forced to attend a three-day retreat at Deep Creek Lake from November 18-20, 1953.

He hadn't wanted to attend. He was having doubts about the ethicality of his work. He didn't need to learn about the results of the work in which he was involved at Camp Detrick, in Frederick. He needed to think and clear his mind.

He knew the men he was sharing the large cabin on the lake with. They were members of the Special Operations Division and the CIA. Vincent Ruwet, Olson's division chief and friend, had picked him up at his house and they had driven west to find this somewhat isolated cabin. It was a large, two-story rental cabin, off of Route 219 about 30 yards from Deep Creek Lake and 100 yards from the nearest neighbor.

The invitation to the "Deep Creek Rendezvous" said that a cover story had been given for the meeting. "CAMOU-FLAGE: Winter meeting of script writers, editors, authors, lecturers, sports magazines."

Olson believed they were there to talk about the joint projects of the Special Operations Division and CIA involving things like biological warfare and using drugs for mind control.

Unbeknownst to Olson, this was also a camouflage story to get him and others to the cabin for an experiment.

The men enjoyed a hearty dinner on Thursday, November

19, and then settled down in the cabin's living room for after-dinner drinks. Robert Lashbrook, a CIA employee and one of the attendees, poured drinks for eight of the men present. He served the drinks and then poured himself and Sidney Gottlieb drinks from a separate bottle, although there was still liqueur in the first. If it struck anyone as odd or if anyone even noticed, no one remarked on it. Olson took the drink offered him. It was a simple choice, but one that would cost him his life.

Frank Olson

He drank the Cointreau and then lost himself in his own thoughts. Sometime between then and Friday afternoon, Olson and the men were told their drinks had been dosed with lysergic acid diethylamide (LSD), according to the Church Committee report. The men wouldn't have noticed it in the

Cointreau because LSD is odorless and colorless. It does have a slightly bitter taste, but the alcohol in the drink would have disguised this.

The men had cause for concern. LSD had been developed in 1938, but its psychedelic properties weren't realized until 1943. Although it is not addictive, it was known to cause delusions, paranoia, and anxiety. The CIA also wanted to know if it could be used for mind control.

When Olson returned home that evening, his wife, Alice, "sensed something was wrong the moment he walked in the door. There was a stiffness in the way he kissed her hello and held her. Like he was doing something mechanical, devoid of any meaning or affection," H. P. Albarelli wrote in *A Terrible Mistake.*

Olson's thoughts now were definitely elsewhere. Later that evening, he admitted to her, "I've made a terrible mistake."

On Monday morning at 7:30 a.m., Olson was waiting for Ruwet when he arrived. Olson admitted his doubts about the work he was doing and said that he wanted to resign.

Olson told his wife later, "I talked to Vin. He said that I didn't make a mistake. Everything is fine. I'm not going to resign.

The next day, Ruwet and Lashbrook convinced Olson to see a psychiatric doctor in New York. Actually, he was meeting with Harold Abramson, an allergist-pediatrician, who was working with the CIA.

Lashbrook and Olson shared a hotel room on the 13th floor of the Statler Hotel. Early in the morning of November 28, a loud crashing noise woke him up. According to the CIA, Olson threw himself out of the window, committing suicide.

The truth turned out to be something far darker and disturbing.

The doorman at the Statler Hotel in New York City had taken a break early around 2:30 a.m. on the morning of November 28, 1953, to go for a drink at the nearby Little Penn Tavern. As he turned a corner, he saw something falling through the air.

"It was like the guy was diving, his hands out in front of him, but then his body twisted and he was coming down feet first, his arms grabbing at the air above him," the doorman told Armond Pastore, the hotel's night manager, according to Albarelli Jr.

The body hit a wooden partition shielding work being done by the hotel and then the sidewalk. Frank Olson was dead.

President Gerald Ford meets with members of the Olson Family to apologize for the actions that led to Frank Olson's death. Photo courtesy of Wikimedia Commons.

The investigation by the CIA, which Olson worked with as part of the Special Operations Unit at Camp Detrick in Frederick, Md., found that Olson had died as "the result of circumstances arising out of [the Deep Creek Lake] experiment," and there was a "direct causal connection between that experiment and his death," according to the CIA's general counsel report, according to *The* (Baltimore) *Sun*.

Although these conclusions had been reached within two weeks of Olson's death, his family was only told that he had died in the course of his work. This allowed the Olson family to collect federal death benefits, while the official results of the death investigation remained classified.

More than 20 years later, a presidential commission investigating CIA activities inside the United States found that an Army scientist had fallen to his death from a hotel room in New York after the CIA had given him LSD in 1953. The Olson family confronted Vincent Ruwet, Olson's division chief and friend, who admitted that the scientist was Frank Olson.

The family then started on a campaign to fully find out what had happened. President Gerald Ford invited the family to the White House and apologized for the death. The family also received a $750,000 settlement from the government.

However, Olson's sons still weren't satisfied that they knew the truth. They had their father's body exhumed in 1994. A new autopsy found that Olson had suffered a blow to the head before he fell from his hotel window. According to the autopsy report, the wound was suggestive of a homicide.

"The Manhattan district attorney's office opened a homicide investigation in 1996. While they were unable to bring charges, they changed the official cause of death from 'suicide' to 'unknown'," *The Sun* reported.

His family filed a lawsuit against the government in 2012, claiming that the CIA is still holding back records about Olson's death.

"The evidence shows that our father was killed in their

custody. They have lied to us ever since, withholding documents and information, and changing their story when con-
venient," said Eric Olson told *The Business Insider*. The lawsuit was dismissed in 2013 when a judge ruled that it had
been "filed too late and is barred under an earlier settlement,"
according to *Bloomberg Business*.

Will the full truth about what happened to Frank Olson
ever be known? It remains to be seen how the journey that
began in a cabin by the lake will end.

Embarrassed Wife Has Doctor Killed

I t's been said that hell hath no fury like a woman scorned. Such fury cost Oakland its first doctor.

When Dr. John Conn stepped off the Baltimore and Ohio Railroad train in 1851, he was a pioneer. Oakland hadn't yet been incorporated as a town, and the region was still a frontier for Maryland. Garrett County didn't even exist yet. It was still a part of Allegany County.

Oakland only had a few hundred citizens, and they needed a doctor. The next-closest physician was Dr. John H. Patterson in Grantsville. To get there and back to Oakland would have taken a full day, and it wouldn't have been a pleasant journey for a sick patient.

Conn set up his office at Second and Oak streets where it quickly flourished.

"In the days before the convenience of a well-stocked pharmacy, it was said that the 'young doctor' either had on hand the correct medication, or could prescribe a suitable home remedy for any attack of ague or vapors, vague ailments which were popular at in that period," according to Garrett County Historical Society book, *Strange and Unusual True Stories of Garrett County.*

Besides the fact that Conn had a monopoly on the medical needs of the community, part of the reason that his practice was successful was that he was young, attractive and people liked him.

Sometimes too much.

Ann Johnson was a woman who believed that she deserved more from life than to work in a general store owned by her older husband, Cornelius, and live in a backwoods town. The general store was on Railroad Street, just 300 feet away from where the Dr. Conn had set up his office. Ann could watch him leaving and entering the building from either the general store or her apartment. Sometimes the young doctor would even come into the store for items.

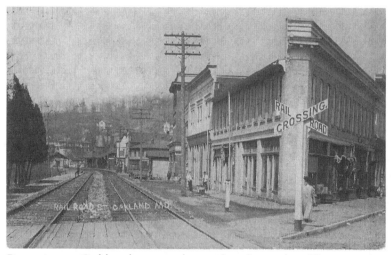

Downtown Oakland near where the doctor's office was located near the turn of the 20th century. Photo courtesy of the Albert and Angela Feldstein Collection.

Ann began to think that Conn might be her way out of Oakland. He was younger than her husband, and he could take her to a city where she could live the life she wanted. She began to find reasons to visit the doctor for treatments for various ailments that either she or her infant daughter, Ida Lucy Florence Jeanette Genevieve Jenny Lind Johnson, supposedly had. She would engage the doctor in conversation to show her sophistication and smile for the single man.

"As time passed, and the visits continued, Mrs. Johnson was convinced that her personality and charm were making an impression on Dr. Conn," according to the Garrett County Historical Society.

And she was making an impression. Conn thought she was quite out of line. He told one person that he thought Ann was a "butterfly fool." When word of this got back to Ann, her dreams collapsed around her. How could this man call her foolish? He could not find a better woman in this town!

Ann stewed on the issue, and her affection for the doctor turned to hate. She said something to Cornelius, most likely accusing Dr. Conn of doing something inappropriate to her during one of her visits.

Then one evening in the spring of 1854, Cornelius left the general store shortly before 7 p.m. and climbed the stairs to his apartment. There he loaded his muzzleloader and took up a position at his window. He watched the doctor approach his office and raised the muzzleloader to his shoulder.

As Cornelius took aim at the doctor's back, Marquis Perry approached the doctor to talk about something.

Cornelius waited for Perry to finish and move on.

"One shot was fired and the doctor crumbled at the step. The bullet passed through his head and lodged in the office door," according to the Garrett County Historical Society.

Perry was so frightened at being next to a murdered man that he ran off. He was found later hiding in his closet. Others, alerted by the shot, came outside and saw the doctor on the ground. They carried him to Thayer's saloon on Railroad Street where Constable Thomas Arnold pronounced Conn dead.

Suspicion quickly fell on Cornelius and Arnold arrested him. However, the only witnesses against him were Perry and Ann. Marquis said he was too shaken to know what happened and Ann wouldn't testify against her husband.

The jury failed to convict Cornelius.

He left Oakland and his wife shortly after that.

Ann, surprisingly, stayed on longer taking care of her daughter. Then one day, she left the young girl in the care of a neighbor, saying that she needed to run some errands. Instead, she boarded a train and never returned to Oakland.

Did Nancy Hufford Kill Three of Her Husbands?

I f looks could kill. Many people thought that Nancy Woodin found a way to make that turn of a phrase come true. Married four times, she must have been attractive enough to catch the eye of many men. The problem was that three of her husbands seemed to die before their time.

Nancy Woodin was the daughter of William and Sally Woodin. William was born in Howard County, but he came to present-day Garrett County to work as an innkeeper and merchant.

Records are not complete about Nancy. At some point, she married John Yeast. He died on July 22, 1833. He left no will, so the court appointed John Layman to administer his estate.

Jacob Brown, a lawyer in the Grantsville area, wrote that Yeast was a young man who had enjoyed "perfect health and strength, yet death came in early manhood and with it grave suspicions of foul play, insidious poison supposed to be the cause of his sudden death., the wife in later years strongly suspected of being the author of his death as well as similar ones."

Only seven months after Yeast's death, Nancy married Layman. Layman, like William Woodin, was a prosperous innkeeper along the National Pike. During her second marriage, Nancy bought a lot along Main Street in Grantsville in her own name. While somewhat unusual for the time, she may have used the inheritance from her father, who had died in 1834, to pay for the purchase.

Nancy's second marriage ended after 11 years when Layman died on September 23, 1845. No suspicions seem to have been raised at the time, and Nancy inherited all of her husband's property.

In 1848, Nancy married for the third time to Samuel Hufford.

"By 1850, she is a woman of considerable wealth; Nancy Woodin Yeast Layman Hufford owned a third of John Yeast's estate, a third of John Layman's property and probably a fourth of her father's," Mrs. John A. Cupler, Sr. wrote in *Journal of the Alleghenies*.

This marriage lasted less than three years as her third husband suffered an untimely death.

It wasn't until the next death that Nancy was connected to that suspicions and accusations arose about Nancy.

When Rebecca Engle became violently ill on September 22, 1851, Nancy came to care for her. Doctors couldn't figure out why the pregnant woman was in such pain. She wasn't miscarrying the baby or going into labor, but she was wasting away.

"Meanwhile, Nancy stayed on 'taking care' of the invalid, carrying medicine, cups of tea and bowls of milk toast which she caused Rebecca to swallow," Cupler wrote.

The baby was eventually born, but Rebecca never recovered from the childbirth. She died a week later.

"Suspicions at once arose in and out of the Engle mansion that there had been foul play," wrote the *Cumberland Evening Times* in a 1907 article about the case.

It was those suspicions that would begin unraveling the questionable deaths in Nancy's life.

Grantsville's black-widow murderess goes on trial

Nancy Hufford had been married three times, and all three of her husbands had died, two of them within a short time after marrying Nancy.

When Rebecca Engle died a week after childbirth, Rebecca's husband, Samuel, was quick to assume that not only had his wife been killed, but Nancy was the murderess. Some researchers have suggested that given how Nancy had benefitted from the deaths of her previous husbands that she was on the lookout for wealthy husband No. 4 and had chosen Samuel Engle. It is not known whether Nancy moved too quickly after Rebecca's death and said something or done something to bring suspicion upon herself, but it came quickly, and Samuel was adamant in his convictions.

He convinced Rebecca's doctor, J. H. Patterson, to disinter Rebecca's body and perform an autopsy. Patterson did so and sent the stomach to Professor Atkin in Baltimore for examination. He could find no evidence of any poison which is not surprising since Rebecca had been dead for weeks by that time.

In the meantime, Nancy was arrested and placed in the Allegany County Jail in September. The following month, she was indicted in Allegany County Circuit Court since Grantsville was still part of Allegany County at that time.

The trial began in November 1851 before Judge Wiesel. State's Attorney and former Maryland Governor Francis Thomas prosecuted the case. Thomas J. McKaig and George A. Pearre defended Nancy.

During the trial, 23 witnesses testified, including five doctors. The state's evidence was called circumstantial. It rested on the fact that Nancy had purchased a lot of arsenic from a store in Grantsville with the remark that she wanted to make a salve for her sore leg. Prosecutors pointed out that she never had a sore leg.

On the other side of the table, the poison could not be found, and Professor Atkin testified that he had found no arsenic in Engle's stomach.

"Who can say the verdict would have been the same if the remaining poison had been produced at the trial? She was acquitted according to the rules of law; but there was hardly one in the whole neighborhood believed her to be innocent," reported the *Cumberland Evening Times*.

The arsenic Nancy purchased eventually was found hidden in a bureau in the Engle house after the trial had ended.

This spurred people to look more into why Nancy had been widowed three times. Two of her four husbands died under mysterious circumstances.

Meanwhile, Nancy disappeared from the public eye. If her goal had been to marry Samuel Engle, she failed miserably. She had even lost most of her own property to pay for the legal defense that had kept her free.

Nancy made one more appearance in the public record when she and Holmes Wiley got a marriage license in 1862.

"The irony was that through his first wife, Elizabeth Yeast, daughter of John Yeast, Nancy had been Holmes Wiley's stepmother-in-law!" Cupler wrote.

When Wiley died in 1878, there was no mention of Nancy in his will, which lead people to believe that she had already died. According to *Findagrave.com*, Nancy is buried in an unmarked grave marked with a field stone in the Wiley Family Cemetery in Grantsville. It appears that Nancy actually outlived her last husband by two years and died in 1880 at the age of 77.

The fact that Nancy lies in an unmarked grave and Wiley didn't leave any part of his estate to his wife makes one wonder what Holmes and his family thought of Nancy. We may never know.

Bank Robbers Get Away
With a Haul From Kitzmiller

A round lunch time on a nice May day, three men walked into Charles Spragne's restaurant in Kitzmiller. Their faces were blackened with cork, and they wore miner's caps. They were unfamiliar to Charles and his wife, but the Spragnes were used to seeing new miners in town from time to time.

Spragne's wife spoke to one of the men, "thinking he was a local miner but did not notice that either of them were masked," *The Republican* reported.

The men finished their lunches, paid their bills, and then walked across the street to the First National Bank of Kitzmiller around 11:45 a.m. As they entered, the men drew large revolvers.

One of the men stepped around Cashier Barclay V. Inskeep's desk and pointed his pistol at Inskeep's face. Sue R. Laughlin, Inskeep's assistant, screamed.

A second man pointed his pistol at Laughlin and told her, "If you scream again. I will kill you."

Laughlin stared at the pistol and then fainted.

With one man covering Inskeep, the other two men quickly gathered what money they could find. Then they cut the wires for the long-distance phone and ran out of the bank, weighed down by the money they were carrying. It was later tallied that the robbers took $9,975.25 with them or roughly $185,000 in today's dollars. One of the men took a bag of nickels, which weighed more than 20 pounds.

In their rush to make their escape, the robbers had not only overlooked $13,000 in paper money that was nearby, but they had also failed to cut the wires for the local telephone at the back of the building.

Inskeep ran out of the bank to the Hamill Coal and Coke Company General Store and reported the robbery. When he ran back outside, he saw the bank robbers starting across the bridge over the Potomac River to Blaine, W.Va. He saw Paul Junkins who was driving a coal company wagon across the bridge to Kitzmiller and called for Junkins to stop the men.

"Junkins climbed from the wagon and told them to stop when one of the men pulled a large revolver from his pocket and commanded him to get back on the wagon and drive on," *The Republican* reported.

Junkins had no wish to be shot, so he obeyed. When he got to Kitzmiller, he was met by a small posse. Junkins got a pistol from one of the men and then joined them in the hunt. Everyone who could carry gun soon joined in the hunt for the bank robbers, including one man who only had a pick handle.

Meanwhile, Inskeep went back to the back and climbed in his car to drive to Elk Garden, W.Va., hoping to head off the robbers.

The robbers continued on their getaway, walking down the Western Maryland Railway tracks about 200 yards and then climbing the bank beside the tracks and heading into the woods. There, they hid among the rocks and fired on the posse as it approached. Junkins who was leading the posse at that point was hit three times—in the arm, the leg, and the forehead. He jumped behind a tree until the robbers stopped firing and fled through the woods again.

The old Kitzmiller Bank. Photo courtesy of the Garrett County Historical Society.

The robbers also shot posse member William Schenk in the hand when he stepped from behind a building at the edge of the woods. During the gunfire exchange, Constable Sharpless from Kitzmiller believed that he had shot one of the men in the chest. A member of the posse accidentally shot Sharpless when he was mistaken for one of the robbers.

A fourth man wearing a red sweater joined the three robbers and led them off through the woods where he had a car running. The men jumped in the car and traded their miner's caps for automobile caps. They sped off up to the mountain toward Elk Garden.

By the time the car raced through Elk Garden, witnesses had reported seeing only three men in the car. They only thought the men were joyriding because news of the robbery hadn't reached the town yet.

Inskeep later told the newspaper, "I do not believe the man who held me up was a professional. Of course I was excited, but believe me, he was trembling all over, too."

He added that the bank and its depositors' wouldn't suffer any loss because the bank carried $15,000 in burglary insurance that would cover the loss.

Four months later, the robbers were finally brought to justice in Woodstock, Va. Paul Neff, Dave Neff, and "Boots" Fry were arrested for different robberies. A group from Kitzmiller, including Inskeep, drove to Woodstock to see if they recognized the men.

"One of the men from the mines identified the Neffs as miners who were at work there until the robbery and then disappeared," *The Republican* reported.

Inskeep also identified the men as the bank robbers.

Car Explosion Kills an Oakland Farmer

C arl Trickett, a 38-year-old electrician, left his work at the Shallmar Powerhouse around 3 a.m. on a cold Saturday morning in January 1935. He drove to his home, a dairy farm two miles west of Oakland, and caught some needed shut eye. The car remained outside his house until he, two of his four children and his housekeeper got into the car on Sunday to drive to Morgantown, W. Va., where Trickett's brother lived.

They never arrived.

Two miles from Terra Alta within sight of the Hopemont Sanitarium, the car exploded. "Small trees and bushes were cut off and mowed down for a distance of 75 feet from the highway by flying particles of the front end of the machine," the *Charlestown Daily Mail* reported.

Trickett was "killed by small bits of the motor as the explosion rocked the entire neighborhood," according to the newspaper. William and Margaret Trickett, ages 12 and 13, were thrown from the car as was Martha Davis, the housekeeper. Davis was killed immediately, but the children survived, battered and bloody.

"A Hopemont worker, first to reach the scene, said the badly bleeding children were attempting to extricate their father from the overturned car, which caught fire," according to the *Charleston Daily Mail*.

The worker helped get Trickett's body out of the debris and

took him to the hospital where he died shortly after arriving.

It quickly became apparent that the explosion hadn't been an accident. Theories began making the rounds as to what had happened, from kerosene replacing the anti-freeze in the radiator to dynamite being placed in the car. The latter proved to be true. "State's Attorney Neil C. Fraley said he believed the dynamite had been placed on Trickett's motor and exploded when the heat became intense enough to set it off," *The (Baltimore) Sun* reported.

Law officers from both West Virginia and Maryland began investigating the explosion. Though the blast had happened in West Virginia, Garrett County Sheriff Clarence Spears investigated because no one knew where or when the explosives might have been planted in the car. Had the dynamite been placed in the car in Shallmar or at the Trickett Farm in Oakland.

The *Cumberland Evening Times* reported that two days after the explosion on Jan. 8 Wallace, Martha Davis' husband Thomas Davis of Shallmar, and Martha's son, were arrested. It wasn't for Martha's murder, though. Wallace had signed his brother-in-law's name to a promissory note to pay for his wife's funeral.

Trickett was buried in Oakland on Jan. 9 and Martha's funeral was in Shallmar on the following day. The Davis men were allowed to attend the funeral, but they had to be accompanied by a deputy. They were returned the jail following the service, not only because of the fraud and forgery, but the newspaper reported that by then they had become suspects in the explosion.

No reason was given for why the Wallaces had become suspects, though the sheriff traveled to Shallmar as part of his investigation. "The trip was made in an effort to check on the theory an enemy of Trickett had hidden dynamite in his automobile while was working in a power plant there," according to the *Cumberland Evening Times*.

Though no resolution to the case can be found, one plausible theory is that Trickett and Davis met while Trickett was doing his work at the Shallmar power plant. Did they have an affair that Wallace found out about and took extreme action to end?

No answer is known, and no one was ever brought to trial for the murder.

A Modern-Day Fagin

C alvin Larch thought that he wasn't getting his hands dirty. He was merely running a junk business and paying for items that customers brought him. At least that is what he told the police.

Not that they believed him.

In early March of 1952, Maryland State Police arrested Larch and nine boys, ranging in age from 12 to 18, for running a burglary and theft ring in the Oakland area.

Larch, who was 29 years old, had moved to Oakland the previous June to work for Sanders Motor Freight as a trucker. He had been involved in an accident earlier in the year, which may have led to him being let go by Sanders.

Larch had been hauling a load of soft drink syrup in the area of Spring Gap, W. Va., during the night. Bright lights from another vehicle temporarily blinded him, and he ran into a 1934 sedan driven by Edith Showalter. She and her husband, James, were injured in the accident, but not seriously. However, the car was totaled, and Larch's truck had $4,000 damage (nearly $36,000 in today's dollars).

Larch had already been running his junk business on the side, but it soon became his sole business.

During this time, the newspaper noted a series of robberies throughout the town that remained unsolved. The high school, NuWay Laundry, Naylor's Store, Garrett Truck and Implement Company, Meyer Motor Sales, and the cars of individuals were all robbed. There seemed to be no connection, and the police had ongoing investigations.

"Spotting a stolen tire which had been marked on a local automobile led to the breaking of the other cases," *The Republican* reported.

With that small thread, police followed leads and made connections that resulted in the 10 arrests. When the Maryland State Police questioned Larch, he admitted that he had purchased batteries, heaters, and tires from the boys. It is not clear whether he admitted to buying other items from the kids that had been stolen, such as guns, knives, shells, and electric drills.

Larch was charged with receiving stolen goods. Although he had admitted his guilt, when he was taken before Magistrate W. O. Bitzer, he pleaded not guilty.

He was held in the county jail in lieu of $2,000 bond.

Meanwhile, the youths in the case faced their own charges. Maryland State Troopers Samuel Conrad and Robert Henline arrested Charles Ashby, 16; Donald Martin, 17; and Perry Lewis, 18. They were charged in the thefts of items from the high school. They pleaded guilty to petty larceny and were given a one-year suspended sentence in the Maryland Reformatory for Males.

The other six boys arrested were not named in the newspaper because they were under 16 years old. However, the newspaper noted that two 15-year-old boys admitted to breaking into Naylor's Hardware and Pontiac and International garages. One of those boys also admitted breaking into the NuWay Laundry with a 13-year-old boy.

Larch was eventually indicted on 30 different counts of theft, larceny, and receiving stolen goods. When he was tried, he was only tried on one of the counts of knowingly receiving stolen property. The state's attorney held the other counts in abeyance, presumably to have the option of trying Larch on them should he be found innocent of the first count.

That wasn't the case, though. After only 10 minutes of deliberation, the jury convicted Larch of knowingly receiving three stolen truck batteries, and he was sentenced to six years in the Maryland State Penitentiary.

Larch appealed his conviction, saying that he had asked for a change of venue and hadn't been given it and also that one of the jurors on the petit jury, Ralph Pritts, had been a prosecution witness.

Associate Judge George Henderson heard the appeal. Larch's lawyers argued that newspaper coverage of the case had biased the jury and his request to have the case moved should have been granted. The prosecution pointed out that in a previous case to have a change of venue, 18 affidavits and numerous newspaper articles about the case had been submitted to support the change, and that hadn't been considered enough. Larch had offered nothing to support his assertions of bias.

As for Pritts being a juror and a witness, Larch's lawyer said, "The actual presence of a single partial man on the sitting jury wipes out the impartiality of the entire body and renders it partial."

The prosecution pointed out that this was not the first time this had happened with Pritts and in the previous case, the defendant whom Pritt testified against had been acquitted by the petit jury.

The original sentence was upheld. Larch went to prison, and Oakland's crime wave ended.

INTERESTING PEOPLE

Einstein's Secret Vacation at Deep Creek Lake

M any people consider Albert Einstein, the smartest man who ever lived. Yet, when this man who knew almost everything needed to unwind one summer, the vacation spot he chose was Deep Creek Lake.

Einstein vacationed for two weeks in September 1946 at the lake. He was seeking a place where he could find an escape from the unwanted media that wrote about how his scientific theories had led to the creation of the atomic bomb.

John Steiding of Midland invited Einstein to vacation at the lake. Steiding was a chemist at the Celanese plant and came to know Einstein through a co-worker's wife, who was sculpting the great man's bust. "Einstein, who wasn't very tall, found it uncomfortable to pose for the artwork since his feet would not touch the floor. John Steiding, being a handyman, made a footstool for Einstein," according to Francis Tam in an article called "Einstein in Western Maryland."

Besides being able to relax out of the national spotlight for awhile, Einstein was also able to have Dr. Frank Wilson examine him for an aneurysm of the aorta of the abdomen.

Einstein stayed at Wilson's lake cottage, the Mar-Jo-Lodge, for two weeks. "He took daily walks along the lake, frequently stopping to chat with strangers who had no idea who he was. He was sometimes seen fishing and also bird-watching with binoculars. He never skipped a meal but was a light eater. He drank a lot of water and lemonade; his favorite vegetable was fresh corn-on-the-cob from Garrett County," Tam wrote.

Robbie Steiding sits on the lap of Albert Einstein during a 1946 visit that Einstein made to Western Maryland. The famous scientist was invited by Robbie's father, John Steiding of Midland, to vacation at Deep Creek Lake. Photo courtesy of Steve James.

In particular, Einstein loved sailing, either with friends or alone. "During one of his many hours spent on the lake with Steiding, Dr. Einstein remarked that 'here you can get nearer to God,'" reported the *Cumberland News*. At times, "people would realize that he wasn't around, go searching for him, and find him in Harry Muma's little sailboat, 'single-handing,' on the Turkey Neck inlet," according to the Garrett County Historical Society's book, *Deep Creek Lake, Past and Present.*

During a visit, John Steiding's brother, Fred, asked Einstein to explain his famous theory of relativity in layman's terms.

"'Put it this way,' said Einstein, 'if you sit on a park bench with your sweetheart, an hour seems like a minute. If you sit on a hot stove by mistake, a minute seems like an hour,'" Tam wrote.

Einstein later said that his vacation at Deep Creek Lake was "one of the most restful and zestful vacations."

When his time at the lake ended, Einstein showed himself to be a generous guest giving Blair Thompson, who had attended him during the vacation, a $50 gratuity, which would equate to more than $1,000 today.

Following the vacation, he was back to work. In October, he wrote the United Nations said the organization should form a world government that maintained peace under the threat of nuclear devastation, according to Ze'ev Rosenkranz in *The Einstein Scrapbook*. Einstein also published his papers on his unified field theory in the 1950's.

To the world, the vacation remained a secret until the *Cumberland News* revealed the story in 1979.

Luck Keeps Deer Park Man Alive During WWII

T he Battle of Leyte Gulf is considered by many to be the largest naval battle during World War II, so it is often forgotten that troops were sent ashore to capture Leyte Island once the gulf was won.

The United States' victory in October 1944 secured the seas around the islands in the Leyte Gulf, but the Japanese still held the islands. On December 7, the 77th Infantry Division, under the command of Major General Andrew Bruce, made an amphibious landing at Albuera, a city on Leyte Island. The 305th, 306th, and 307th Infantry Regiments came ashore without incident, but that peace wouldn't last.

Kamikaze attacks sunk U.S. destroyers. Japanese troops on the island regrouped and began fighting back against the Americans. Private Denver C. Sharpless of Deer Park was among the U.S. troops taking fire.

He had been overseas for a year after having gone through basic training at Fort Jackson in South Carolina. He had enlisted in the army at Fort Meade in April 1942 for the "duration of the War or other emergency, plus six months," which was a standard enlistment for WWII.

The 30-year-old infantryman had just taken cover in a ditch during a firefight when he saw a Japanese soldier emerge from his cover.

"He was the biggest Jap I ever saw," Sharpless told an interviewer while he was in the hospital recovering from a nerve ailment in his right leg. "Must have been more than six feet and I'm not exaggerating when I say that his head was as big as one of our helmets."

Japanese snipers who were killed by U. S. forces during the Battle for Leyte. Photo courtesy of Wikimedia Commons.

The average height of Japanese soldiers during the war was under five feet five inches. Sharpless himself was only five feet eight inches tall and weighed 152 pounds.

33

He wasn't too scared of the Japanese solider. Sharpless had found cover, and he had his rifle. And that big, hulking soldier made an easy target.

Then the Japanese soldier saw Sharpless and dropped out of sight. The soldier began crawling, and Sharpless saw him again when he passed through an open area 25 yards away.

"Then I began to get frightened because, when I pulled the trigger, my M1 wouldn't fire," Sharpless said. "I yanked open the bolt and saw that the firing pin was broken."

Sharpless was considering scurrying away, so he didn't fall within the soldier's sights. Then he saw another American with a Browning Automatic Rifle coming toward him. The American soldier had also seen the Japanese soldier.

Sharpless asked to borrow the man's rifle, but the soldier told him that he wanted to take out the Japanese soldier. He fired a couple shots, and the Japanese soldier went down.

"I wished at the time that I had a camera to take his picture," Sharpless said. "He looked like one of those oversize freaks you see in comic strips."

Besides fighting at Leyte, Sharpless also fought on Guam. He earned the Combat Infantry Badge for exemplary conduct under fire and the Philippines Liberation campaign ribbon. Despite surviving enemy fire, the nerve ailment manifested itself a few months later. Its severity required that he be sent to a California hospital for treatment.

He was the son of Robert and Bertha Sharpless. His parents had divorced when he was young, though, and his mother had raised Sharpless in Deer Park. His father was a coal miner who lived in Swanton and had remarried.

Denver Sharpless died in Ohio in 1991.

Grantsville's Grand Old School Teacher Returns

After the Civil War ended, a young 24-year-old veteran returned home and decided that he wanted to be a teacher. He found a job as the schoolmaster for the school in Grantsville, which was then part of Allegany County. Ross R. Sanner was a man who had commanded men in battle, and he turned those leadership skills toward educating a new generation of young citizens.

"The writer (editor of the Republican) had the privilege of being one of his primary pupils in 1868 and among the readers of The Republican are many who received their first instructions from this grand old pedagogue and who have ever since held him in grateful memory and high esteem," Benjamin Sincell wrote in 1916.

Sanner was born in Lower Turkeyfoot Township in Somerset County, Pa., in 1842. He had answered the call for soldiers in 1861 and walked to Uniontown, Pa., to enlist in the 85th Regiment Pennsylvania Infantry as a 19-year-old private. He fought gallantly in various campaigns with his unit and soon started earning promotions, ending the war as a captain.

He was wounded at Folly Island in Charleston, S.C., and spent two months recovering in a hospital. He returned to duty and was injured a second time during the Battle of Petersburg in Virginia.

During the fight, Sanner was fighting alongside his

cousin, Norman Ream, when Ream was injured.

"He was six feet, two inches tall, and Captain Sanner carried him a mile on his shoulder to safety, the *Cumberland Press* reported. "Later Captain Sanner was wounded in the same battle and the pair became separated."

It was this wound that caused him to be honorably discharged from the army on September 22, 1864, and he began collecting an invalid pension.

Grantsville School before 1909. Photo courtesy of Alice Eary.

Upon his return home, he attended the Iron City Business College in Pittsburgh and Mount Union College in Mount Union, Ohio. In 1866, he became a teacher in Grantsville, and also a husband when he married Alice C. Fuller.

He eventually moved on to teach in schools in Frostburg; Cumberland; Confluence, Pa.; and at the Soldiers' Orphans' School in Uniontown.

Sanner moved to North Dakota for a number of years to try his hand at wheat farming, but teaching was his passion, and he returned to the area once again and became the superintendent of schools in Oakland.

Then in 1915, his career came full circle and returned to Grantsville to once again become the principal. He and his wife took up residence at the Casselman Hotel, and Sanner enjoyed teaching with fewer responsibilities.

"In times of peace as well as of war he has stood by the best principles of government, and his influence over the minds of his pupils and those coming within his sphere has always been exerted for good," according to *Portrait and Biographical Record of the Sixth Congressional District of Maryland in 1898.*

Three years after his return to his teaching roots, "Grantsville's Grand Old School Teacher" passed away in Confluence at 76 years old from cirrhosis of the liver. He was buried at the Confluence Baptist Cemetery.

A 10-Pound Boy Named "Oxygen"

M rs. Hutson screamed with the final effort to push her son into the world on June 12, 1932. Exhausted, she collapsed back onto her bed that was now damp with the sweat of her labor. The doctor announced that the baby was a boy. He cut the umbilical cord and swatted the child on the bottom to start him crying.

The cries started, but they were weak, not the full-throated wail a 10-pound baby should have been able to make.

Though undiagnosed at the time, the baby may have had transient tachypnea. While in the womb, babies get their oxygen from the blood vessels of the placenta. Their lungs are full of fluid. They begin to clear the fluid in response to hormonal changes shortly before they are born. More fluid is squeezed out of their lungs during the birthing process, and the remainder gets coughed out after birth. A baby with transient tachypnea clears his lungs too slowly, causing breathing difficulties. The child breathes harder and faster trying to get enough oxygen.

This is what was happening with the newborn baby.

When Mrs. Hutson asked to hold her newborn son, the doctor said that she would have to wait.

Kitzmiller, where the Hutsons lived, was one of the larger coal-mining towns along the Upper Potomac in 1932. In its heyday, the town had a bank, bakery, theater, hotel, post office, and stores, but it never had a hospital.

However, a hospital is what the baby needed. While in most instances a home birth wouldn't be a problem, it was now. The baby was struggling to breathe and without the right equipment, the type of equipment found at a hospital, the little guy might not survive.

L.C. Hutson, far right, used his experience with mine rescue equipment to help save the life of his newborn son in 1932. Photo courtesy of *www.whilbr.com*.

The closest hospital was Miner's Hospital in Frostburg, but the doctor worried the baby might not survive the journey.

L.C. Hutson, the baby's father, was a vocational mining instructor and he had another idea. The baby needed oxygen, and Hutson knew how to get it. He and the doctor placed a call to Mine Inspector Powers and Assistant Vocational Mining Instructor Ewing in Frostburg. They brought an inhalator from the Frostburg Mine Rescue Station to Kitzmiller.

"A surgeon and nurse were present and Messrs. Powers and Ewing, assisted by Mr. Hutson, gave oxygen to the babe and revived him," reported the *Cumberland Sunday Times.* "The babe, a fine 10-pound boy, has been nicknamed 'Oxygen,' a memorial to the occasion."

Garrett County would eventually get a hospital, but not until Oxygen was an adult in 1950. That is when George W. Loar bequeathed $175,000 to Garrett County to build a hospital. The Garrett County Memorial Hospital was a 30-bed facility with an emergency room, laboratory, X-ray department and operating room when it first opened.

Five years later, 20 more beds were added to accommodate the growing need for hospital services in the region.

Story update: Charles "Oxygen" Hutson is now a great-grandfather in his 80s who has been married for more than55 years. He splits his time between west Texas and Garrett County.

John Garrett Used the Railroad to Help the Union

T he Baltimore and Ohio Railroad was one of the Union's greatest weapons during the Civil War. It wasn't a weapon of destruction but of transportation. The United States had 200 railroads when the war began. Most of them were in the North. Also, the distinctive thing about the Northern railroads was that most of them had a uniform distance between their rails. This allowed the Union to move troops and goods faster and with fewer transfers than the Confederacy could.

Even among the Northern railroads, the B&O was special. At the beginning of the war, the B&O had 513 miles of track that ran from Washington, DC, to Wheeling, Virginia.

"From Wheeling, the train would be taken across the river on floats to Parkersburg," said Courtney Wilson, executive director of the B&O Railroad Museum in Baltimore. From there, connections could be made to other railroads, but the Washington, DC, connection was the critical one. Regarding rail service, the B&O was Washington's lifeline to the Union.

While the right-of-way of the railroad made it useful for moving troops along the front, part of it ran through areas that at times were under Confederate control. The Southern troops recognized the advantage the B&O gave the Union and often targeted it for destruction. Over the course of the war, 143 raids and battles involved the B&O.

John Garrett, president of the B&O Railroad during
the Civil War and the man for whom Garrett County
is named. Photo courtesy of Wikimedia Commons.

"Millions and millions and millions of dollars of damage
was done to the railroad during the war," Wilson said.

The Union also recognized the importance that keeping the railroad running meant to the war effort. Brigades were stationed on the eastern and western ends of the rail line and were dedicated to protecting the B&O from not only regular Confederate Army actions but also raids from the growing number of ranger units.

John W. Garrett was president of the B&O during from 1858 until he died at his summer home in Deer Park in 1884. He was a Virginian by birth, and he continued to treasure his birth state even after it seceded from the Union.

"His loyalties were in question at first because he had called the B&O a Southern railroad," Wilson said. He also referred to Confederate leaders as "our Southern friends."

However, Garrett realized that his financial future lay with a Union victory in the war. Once he realized this, Garrett became a staunch Unionist. Besides, allowing the army to transport troops on the railroad, he allowed telegraph lines to be strung along the railroad's right of way to facilitate communication.

His support of the Union could clearly be seen before the Battle of Monocacy in 1864. Railroad agents began reporting Confederate troop movements a week and a half before the action. Garrett passed the information on to Gen. Lew Wallace who was in charge of the Union defense. He also made sure that trains carried munitions and troops to the area.

It was a win-win situation for both the railroad and the Union. The Union was able to move its men and equipment quickly to where they were most needed. Garrett got army protection for the railroad and lucrative government contracts.

The B&O went on to play a major role throughout the war from being attacked during John Brown's raid on Harper's Ferry to transporting President Lincoln's body back to Illinois after his assassination.

Although Garrett did not live in Garrett County, he enjoyed vacationing there. He saw its potential as a resort destination for city dwellers seeking to escape the heat of the summer. Of course, to make the journey from the sweltering urban areas to the mountain paradise, they would use his railroad.

John Garrett's summer home in Deer Park. Garrett is on the porch with his wife. His son, John, is on the high-wheel bike and son Horatio is on the second-floor porch. Photo courtesy of Western Maryland's Historical Library.

After the Civil War ended, Garrett purchased a 300-acre tract called "Plenty and Peace" that adjoined Deer Park. There, in view of the railroad, he built a Swiss-chalet style hotel that opened on July 4, 1873.

Although primarily to service train passengers, it soon became a tourist destination. It was so successful that two 50-room annexes had to be added nine years later. Cottages were also added.

"This was the period in which wealthy families from Baltimore, Washington, Pittsburgh, Philadelphia and even Cincinnati and St. Louis were accustomed to come to Deer

Park on the fast through passenger trains, all of which stopped at the hotel's own railroad station. They brought their own servants and many of them rented cottages for the season. Also, in box cars, came their horses and carriages and – much later, before the day of the hard surfaced roads – their Packards, Wintons, Pierce-Arrows, Panhard-Levassore, Locomobiles and other fine automobiles," according to a 1970 article in *The Glades Star*.

Garrett also had a 15-room summer home built for his own family to enjoy the county that had been named after him.

A postcard drawing of the Deer Park Hotel built by John Garrett as a railroad hotel. Photo courtesy of the Garrett County Historical Society.

Garrett County had formed from Allegany County in 1872. The Rev. Richard Browning is credited with selecting Garrett County from the suggested names. He and many citizens felt that Garrett had done a lot to promote the region not only because of his railroad but his personal efforts to help the area.

For instance, when the B&O Railroad Station opened in Oakland in 1884, it fulfilled a promise that Garrett had made that if Oakland were named Garrett County's county seat, he would build a train station befitting a county seat.

Although Garrett did not live in Garrett County, he died there. He passed away on September 26, 1884, at his summer home in Deer Park.

The B&O Railroad Station in Oakland. Photo courtesy of Wikimedia Commons.

The Lost World of Leo J. Beachy

"**M**y camera lens does not lie. It took just what it saw, no more, no less," Leo J. Beachy once wrote.

His camera captured faces and scenes of Garrett County in the early 20th century. Horse-drawn wagons. One-room log schoolhouses. Historic building that have since been destroyed. Weddings and school classes. Dirt roads and mud streets.

"Of all the early Maryland photographers whose work I have seen," photographer Marion E. Warren said in *The Eye of the Beholder: Photographs by Marion E. Warren 1940-1988*, "Leo Beachy had a sensitivity for human interest that was unique."

It is a world that now lives only in the memories of the oldest citizens and for decades after Beachy's death in 1927, it was believed as lost as the time that had spawned it.

"My Life as a Backwoods Schoolteacher"

Leo Beachy was born in 1874 on a farm called Mt. Nebo near Grantsville. He was the seventh of 10 children born to Jonas Beachy and Anna Youtzy. Beachy lived on the family farm his entire life never marrying or having children.

As an adult, he became a school teacher, teaching in small one-room schoolhouses, such as Negro Mountain School, Engle School, and Compton School.

"He wrote an article called 'My Life as a Backwoods School Teacher.' It was so sad to read. He was very unhappy," his niece, Maxine Beachy Broadwater said.

47

According to the book, *Legacy of Leo J. Beachy*, Beachy won a small Kodak camera as a sales premium from E. L. Kellogg & Co. With this camera, he took his first picture. It was of his mother staring up at the sun.

One of Leo Beachy's pictures of the Cove. Photo courtesy of the Garrett County Historical Society.

"When he developed the picture, he wrote, 'Lo and behold, I thought I was Rembrandt,'" Broadwater said, recalling some of her uncle's writings.

His interest in photography sparked, he soon found himself a larger camera that took pictures on glass plates. However, he didn't do much with it at the time and stored it away in a trunk.

"What induced me to take up photography was that I wanted our home photographer to go to that old log school where I taught my first school and take some pictures of it and the great hills lying about it and the rocky Savage River. He never got the pictures for me," Beachy wrote.

He remembered his camera and took the picture himself.

Pleased with the results, he began taking other pictures of classes, places, and people of Garrett County.

Beachy suffered from a crippling disease that caused him to give up teaching. Today, the disease can be identified as multiple sclerosis, though it did not have a name at the time.

He threw his work efforts into photography.

"The Bullock tractor" by Leo Beachy. Photo courtesy of the Garrett County Historical Society.

"Aunt Kate would carry him on her back to the wagon and get him on. Then he would drive to where he needed to be, and someone there would carry him off," Broadwater said.

Over the next two decades, it's not known how many glass-plate photos that Beachy took, but the estimates are in the tens of thousands. He also began making a national name for himself. *Motor Trend* ran some of his National Road photos in 1925, and *National Geographic* ran at least one of his photos in 1926 of a Garrett County snow scene.

Former President Theodore Roosevelt also admired Beachy's work when he judged a photography contest.

Beachy had entered a picture of "Speedy" Bittinger on his motorcycle and sidecar delivering mail along the National Road and won the national competition.

Beachy died from complications of multiple sclerosis on May 5, 1927. He was only 53 years old. He is buried in Otto Cemetery, near Grantsville.

Leo J. Beachy and children. Photo courtesy of the Garrett County Historical Society.

A legacy lost

Broadwater was only six years old when she helped her brothers load boxes of her uncle's glass plates onto a wagon to clean out Beachy's studio so that it could be converted into a chicken house.

"I still feel guilty about it today, but I was young, and I did what I was told," Broadwater said.

The glass plates were taken to a creek and dumped into it where they shattered.

Luckily, Beachy had been a prolific photographer, and the boxes dumped into the river were not the only boxes of his photographs.

A legacy found

In 1975, a friend came into the Grantsville Library where Broadwater worked and showed her a set of 75 glass-plate negatives.

"The minute I saw them I knew they were Uncle Leo's," Broadwater said.

A shot of people gathering hay by Leo Beachy. Photo courtesy of the Garrett County Historical Society.

Then a few years later a man who was renting the property next to the old stone Casselman River Bridge, commented to Broadwater that he wished that Dr. Alta Shrock, the founder of Penn Alps, would get rid of the boxes of old glass plates in the old wash house. The boxes were so heavy that they were collapsing the old shelves they were sitting on.

Broadwater called Shrock, who gave her the plates, around 2,500 of them. They had been rescued from a dump many years before, stored away, and forgotten. Kate Beachy had apparently held back some of her brother's glass plates to preserve them. She eventually forgot about them, and when she moved to New York, the new owners of the house found the boxes of glass plates and took them to the dump. Luckily, someone realized they had historical value and rescued them, although he, too, eventually forgot them.

A snow scene where the Oakland Road (MD Route 219) meets National Highway (US Route 40) by Leo Beachy. Photo courtesy of the Garrett County Historical Society.

Since that time, Broadwater has worked hard to preserve her uncle's legacy by caring for the glass plates and displaying the scenes captured on them.

"I never met Uncle Leo, but I feel as though I know him though working on the glass-plate negatives," Broadwater said.

Her efforts had paid off as he uncle's talent has come to be appreciated.

In his book, *Maryland Time Exposures, 1840-1940*, William Stapp, curator of photography at the National Portrait Gallery, wrote, "Beachy's photographs are entrancing pictures, composed with naïve charm ... (They) are compelling, summoning up visions of a style of life blessed by innocence ... They reassure us about our past, and thus give us comfort for the present and for the future. That is no mean accomplishment for an unpretentious small-town photographer."

"Blessed is the man that enjoyeth rest" by Leo Beachy. Photo courtesy of the Garrett County Historical Society.

Remembering Leo Beachy

You can view a documentary about Beachy, "Leo Beachy: A Legacy Nearly Lost", on the Garrett County Historical Society website. The documentary originally aired on WQED in Pittsburgh.

Life Magazine also published many of his photos in 1990 in a 10-page feature. You can view many of the photographs on the Garrett County Historical Society website or by visiting the Grantsville Museum.

The Maryland Historical Society also has a small collection of Beachy's glass-plate negatives that it acquired in 2010.

Broadwater has also published four volumes of small books with hundreds of Beachy's photographs reprinted in them. The Garrett County Commissioners proclaimed the week of July 5-11 as "Leo Beachy Week" in Grantsville. Besides the proclamation, there was a reception and other special events held throughout the week.

The Casselman River Bridge in Grantsville. Photo courtesy of the Garrett County Historical Society.

"Buck" Broadwater Comes Down from the Mountain

"**B**uck" Broadwater had lived in the mountains above Bond all of his life. He'd been to Piedmont, W. Va., once as a youngster, but that was it for his travels. He was happy on the mountain. It was the only life he knew.

"He had seen Baltimore and Ohio Railroad trains occasionally on the Seventeen-Mile Grade but had never traveled by rail," *The Republican* reported in 1938. The Seventeen-Mile Grade is a steep section of railroad track between Piedmont and Altamont. At points along the grade, the slope is more than 2.5 percent as the track descends 1,700 along the way. The steep grade caused concern among railroaders because trains moving down the track tended to pick up speed and were hard to slow down.

The railroad had a shipping point at Bond to carry the logs and lumber from the logging companies located there.

It's not certain whether Broadwater's isolation was self-imposed out of disinterest in leaving his mountain cabin or imposed upon him by his father and two brothers with whom he lived.

Whatever the reason, everything changed on January 7, 1938, when Garrett County officials drove up the mountain to bring Broadwater to Oakland. The newspaper pointed out that although Broadwater was 31 years old, this was his first ride in a car.

"Relief workers, health nurses and neighbors had reported him as undernourished, more or less mentally undeveloped and not properly cared for in the primitive home where he resided with his father and two brothers," *The Republican* reported.

While this may have been true, it didn't dampen Broadwater's spirits. By all accounts, he quickly got over the novelty of riding in a car and simply enjoyed the scenery.

"When shown an electric light in the sheriff's office and told to "put it out," he blew at it as he would have done to extinguish an oil lamp or candle in his home," the newspaper reported. "He was much puzzled at his inability to affect the light until shown the switch that controlled everything."

In Oakland, Broadwater was tested to determine whether he should be committed to an institution where he could receive proper care and treatment.

Broadwater even told State's Attorney Neil Fraley that "I'm too dumb to know much."

This caused Fraley to joke that Broadwater must be a Democrat. Broadwater shook his head and said that he couldn't remember. Then a Democrat who was at the meeting suggested that Broadwater was Republican.

Broadwater piped up, "That's it; that's what I am—a Republican."

ACCIDENTS, DISASTERS, AND ILLNESS

The Sneeze That Killed

Elmer Martin, who lived near Crellin, returned to work on October 15, 1918, after being sick for a few days. The 28-year-old felt fine and needed to get back to earning a living at the Turner-Douglas Mine as a driver.

He seemed fine his first day back, but when he didn't report to work the next day, someone realized that he had never made it home. A search began and lasted all night until Martin's body was discovered alongside the tracks of the Preston Railroad.

He had apparently just fallen down and died.

He wasn't the only one, either. Across Garrett County, more than 100 people were killed from Spanish Flu in fall of 1918. The flu wasn't just a problem in the county, either. Spanish Flu reached nearly every place on the globe, and by the time it subsided at the end of November, an estimated 50 million people had died from it.

One physician wrote that patients rapidly "develop the most vicious type of pneumonia that has ever been seen" and later when cyanosis appeared in patients "it is simply a struggle for air until they suffocate." Another doctor said that the influenza patients "died struggling to clear their airways of a blood-tinged froth that sometimes gushed from their mouth and nose."

The flu seemed to sneak up of Garrett County officials. At first, the many illnesses and deaths were written off as the result of a typical flu outbreak. Many areas in the country began seeing the effects of the flu in late September. In Garrett County, an increase in the number of deaths could be seen, but there was no mention of a problem with Spanish Flu.

Police officers in Washington State wearing masks to try and keep from catching the flu. Photo courtesy of Wikimedia Commons.

Then on October 8, U.S. Surgeon General Rupert Blue sent a telegram to county officials ordering all public meetings, public places of amusement, and schools to be closed. "The order is drastic and was promulgated for the purpose of conserving the public health. Its effect will be to close all churches, Sunday schools and all manner of gatherings," the *Republican* reported.

These restrictions were actually mild compared to some areas. Washington, D.C., San Francisco, and San Diego passed laws forcing their citizens to wear gauze masks when outdoors. Some towns required a signed certificate of health if someone wanted to enter the city.

The flu caused a domino effect in various professions. Many doctors had been drafted to fight in World War I, which was winding down at the time. So there was already a shortage of doctors when the increase in flu patients added to their workload. They were exposed to the sick more frequently, and many of the remaining doctors took ill themselves. This further increased the workload on the healthy doctors and increasing their chances of exposure to the flu. This happened in Accident, where the town's sole doctor, Robert Ravenscroft, fell ill with the flu.

Similar things happened with nurses and gravediggers as well.

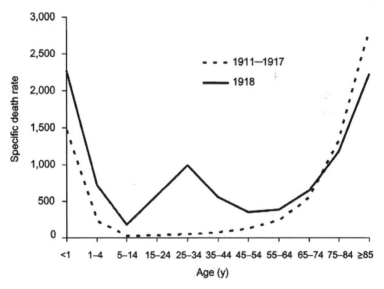

The chart shows the ages of people who died from the Spanish Flu. Unlike the U-shaped curve of the typical flu, Spanish Flu had a W shape. Photo courtesy of Wikimedia Commons.

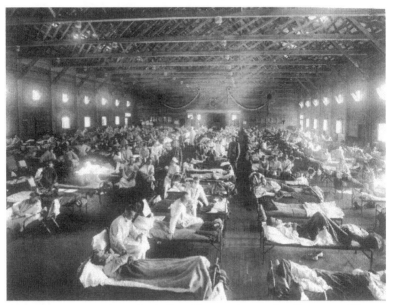

An emergency hospital for flu patients in Kansas. Photo courtesy of Wikimedia Commons.

An article in the *Journal of the Alleghenies* read, "Bodies of Frostburg servicemen stationed at Fort Meade were sent back to Frostburg wrapped in blankets and tagged. Their bodies were stored temporarily in the corner house where the Frostburg Legion building now stands. Behind the post office in a carriage house, open doors revealed bodies laid on the floor. At the Durst Funeral Home from October 5 to October 31, 1919, ninety-nine bodies were prepared for the last rites. Those bodies, placed in rough caskets or wooden boxes, were carted to the cemetery and stacked until burial."

Among those people who were buried, *The Republican* noted that by the middle of the month all funerals were required to be private.

For the next couple weeks, the obituaries of people who died from Spanish Flu took up two columns or more in *The Republican*. The Oct. 17 headline read "Death List Is Most

Appalling Many Fall Victims of the Plague Sweeping the Country".

In Allegany County, the Baltimore and Ohio Railroad had 6,000 employees in the county and 1,000 reported sick with the flu on October 4. At its peak, 60 percent of the B&O workers were out sick with the flu.

After one month in Philadelphia, the flu had killed nearly 11,000 people, including almost 800 people on October 10, 1918.

Every Garrett County business suffered. Coal production fell off because so many miners were sick. Even getting a telephone call through was harder because operators were out sick.

Neither the county or state health departments have precise numbers on how many people died from the flu because the cause of death did not have to be reported. The estimate would be between 100 and 150 people died in Garrett County among a population of less than 20,000.

The Spanish Flu is one of the reasons health departments across the country began collecting that type of information. However, even if that information had been gathered, overworked doctors didn't always fill out death certificates for their patients because too many patients who were still living needed their attention.

Spanish Flu killed more people than died in World War I and in a shorter time frame, too, yet the war captured the headlines during 1918. Estimates are 675,000 Americans died from the Spanish Flu or ten times more than died in the war.

Spanish Flu killed more people in one year than the Black Plague did in four years.

Spanish Flu was so devastating that human life span was reduced by ten years in 1918.

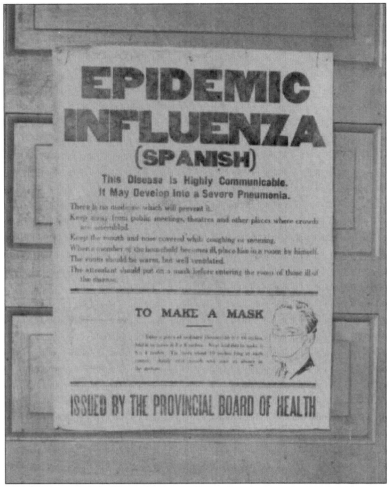

A typical quarantine notice that was posted on the homes of families that contracted Spanish Flu in 1918. Photo courtesy of Wikimedia Commons.

By the time the flu began to subside in Garrett County at the end of the October, the newspaper notes that it had "visited nearly every abode in Garrett county, leaving death and desolation in its wake." At this time, Oakland's new cases and deaths were on the decline while the small Potomac Valley town had yet to reach their peak, though the growth in new cases was slowing. Also, *The Republican* notes that although everywhere in the county was hit with cases of the flu, "Some sections of the county have been particularly fortunate in not have a case of influenza with its resultant fatal termination. Especially is this true of Accident, Bittinger and the town of Grantsville."

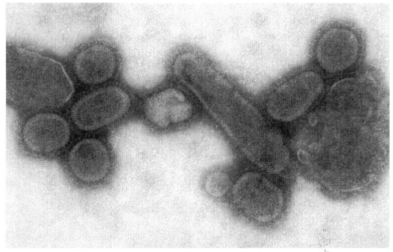

The Spanish Flu virus. Photo courtesy of Wikimedia Commons.

Spanish Flu is the deadliest plague that has ever struck the world and yet, it remains largely forgotten either through the selective memories of the people who lived through it or because history books remember World War I and not the flu.

Whatever the reason, October 1918 remains the month that the world mourned.

Mayor Dies of Heart Attack During Meeting

M embers of the Oakland Fire Department were meeting on Tuesday, February 17, 1948, at City Hall. The discussion went back and forth with the members of the fire department pushing the need for a new firehouse and community building. While it was a lively debate, no one was getting angry or worked up.

Mayor Alexander George Hesen was recognized and stood up to address the group about the topic. Before he could say anything, he suddenly collapsed to the floor. Those present tried to use an inhalator to revive him, but it didn't work.

Dr. E. I. Baumgartner, who happened to be the president of the city council, was called to the meeting room. He examined the mayor and pronounced him dead. The cause was determined to be a heart attack that had killed him almost instantly.

Although Hesen had been ill for several months from a heart condition, he was thought to be on the mend. His doctor had urged him to rest and curtail his activities, which he had done. The fire department meeting was the first evening meeting that he had attended in weeks, according to *The Republican*.

Hesen was only 53 years old at the time of his death. He had been born in Keyser, W. Va., in 1894 and moved to Oakland at an early age. As an adult, he had joined the army and served overseas during World War I. When he returned to Oakland at the end of the war, he opened and operated the

Hesen Garage and Service Station.

He had just been finishing up his first two-year term as mayor of Oakland when he died.

Alex Hesen after he enlisted in the army during World War I. Photo courtesy of the Garrett County Historical Society.

"He had told friends he would be a candidate for re-election next month," *The Republican* reported. He had also served two two-year terms on the city council.

He had been elected in March 1946 when he ran unopposed for mayor. At that time, long-time Mayor Lawrence M. Fraley had decided not to run for re-election. He had served as Oakland's mayor from 1924 to 1930 and then from 1938 to 1946 and wanted to run for Maryland State Senate (a position that he won).

Hesen's funeral was held February 20 at St. Peter's Catholic Church. Rev. Zinkand officiated at the Mass and Hesen was interred in the Oakland Cemetery.

Joseph Hinebaugh was elected as the Mayor of Oakland in March and served in that position until 1956.

Hesen was survived by his widow, Florence, and three sons—James, Robert, and William. When William died in 2012, the *Cumberland Times-News* noted that "he was the last surviving member of the Hesen Family residing in Garrett County."

Boy Crashes Through Ice on the Little Yough

With the cold temperatures during the winter of 1926, rivers froze and children bundled up when they ventured outside. Seven-year-old Bobby Tibbetts of Oakland was one of those children. With his hat, mittens, and coat on, he hurried outside to play with his friends.

He saw his friends on the other side of the Little Youghiogheny River to the south of Oakland. The other boys waved him over. Bobby was hesitant to cross the river, but his friends assured him that they had done it. Fears assuaged, Bobby hurried across the ice.

Midway across the stream, it cracked, and Bobby disappeared below the surface with a loud splash. He fell into one of the deepest points of the river located about 100 yards above the dam at Oakland Mill. Bobby quickly bobbed to the surface, screaming, and clung to the edge of the ice.

His friends called for help. Three men on their side of the river – Paul Beckwith, Elmer Shaffer, and Samuel Butler – rushed up and saw what had happened.

They set about to try and help Bobby immediately. They didn't know how long he could remain conscious before hypothermia set in, but they knew the water was freezing cold and making the young boy's body temperature lower every second.

The fact that Bobby was screaming, shivering, and clinging to the ice was a good sign. Some of the signs of hypothermia include drowsiness, slurred speech, loss of coordination, and shivering that eventually stops.

The men knew that they couldn't go out on the ice. It hadn't held Bobby's weight so it most likely wouldn't hold any of them.

One of the men found a board and laid it on the ice, but it was too short to reach the young boy.

Ernest Townshend, Bobby's grandfather, approached Bobby from the side of the river that Bobby had originally been on. He had been in his house on Water Street when he heard the screams for help.

"When the little fellow's head began to droop it needed only a call from Mr. Townshend 'to hang on and the men would reach him,' to bring him erect and redouble the strength of his grip on the ice," *The Republican* reported.

A rope was then found and brought to the river. One end was tossed to Bobby who struggled to grip it because his hands were growing stiff. The men pulled on the rope slowly and steadily so that Bobby wouldn't lose his grip. The river reluctantly released the boy, and the men pulled him to shore.

"He was immediately taken to Mr. Butler's home and given a vigorous rub-down and later taken to his own home on Water street where he was further cared for," *The Republican* reported. Bobby lived in his grandfather's house with his mother, infant brother, grandmother, aunts, uncles and cousins.

Then entire rescue had taken 15 minutes. Depending on how cold the water was, it was long enough to have killed a person, particularly a child who had less body mass. Bobby survived, though.

The newspaper reported that he seemed to suffer no ill effect from his experience in the river than a slight stiffness in his legs.

Train Crashes Into County Bus Killing Seven Children

H aving no children of his own, 49-year-old Leroy Campbell enjoyed the laughter and squeals of the children he drove to and from school each day, but it was their screams of terror that would haunt him for the rest of his life.

Campbell had a perfect driving record, and he had driven a school bus for the Garrett County Board of Education for eight years by 1959. He picked up children in the Loch Lynn and Mountain Lake Park areas and delivered them to Southern High School and Dennett Road Elementary each day school was in session.

On the morning of September 10, 1959, Campbell picked up 27 students and headed towards the schools where he would drop them off. As he crossed the railroad tracks at Route 560 in Loch Lynn, the bus stalled.

He was attempting to restart the engine when the crossing lights started flashing, and the bells started ringing. Campbell looked up and saw the eastbound Diplomat passenger train from St. Louis fast approaching on its way to Washington going 50 mph, which was the legal limit.

Roy Dixon, a 12-year-old student on the bus, said later, "I'll never forget the look on Mr. Campbell's face. He looked like he was scared to death. But he's a good driver and he helped to get some of the kids off the bus."

Campbell ordered the children off the bus through the

front door. Campbell said the rear exit was not opened because it would have let the students out right on the railroad tracks.

The accident scene after a school bus from Loch Lynn was hit by a train at a railroad crossing. Photo courtesy of the Garrett County Historical Society.

"Everybody knew the train was going to hit us. Everybody wanted to get out. Everybody rushed to the doors of the bus all at once. One girl, she got stuck in the door. I didn't know what to do. Finally, somebody pushed her out," Roy said.

Delores Shaffer was the girl pinned in the door until someone pulled her free. She and eight other children managed to get off the bus.

Engineer Otto Droege saw the bus and thought it would cross over the tracks. When he realized it was stalled, he applied the emergency brakes of the train. The train lurched, and the brakes squealed.

Roy said, "I grabbed [my younger sister, Gladys] by the

hand and we jumped. I ran down the track and saw fire flying from the wheels of the engine. Then I looked back and saw the train hit. There was a big cloud of dust, then kids came flying out through the windows."

The train quickly slowed, but it was still going 20 mph when it hit the bus and pushed it down the track until it wrapped around a utility pole.

"The train hit and it jerked me," Mary Ellen Itnyre, a 14-year-old student on the bus said later. "I was knocked under the front seat. There was a lot of dust and it was dark and I thought the train was carrying me away with it. All I could hear after the crash was the moaning and groaning from the rest of the kids in the school bus."

Phyllis Paugh lived in an apartment next to crash scene. When she heard the crash, she ran outside to see what had happened. "When I got outside, I got a little weak. There were children screaming...some had blood on them...they were crying, and there was a lot of confusion. The children's bodies were scattered along the track. Some were hurt, but some of them looked dead. They were lying along the tracks from the crossing where the train hit, down to where the bus had stopped," Paugh said.

Seven ambulances and two station wagons quickly responded to the scene. Some of the vehicles couldn't speed while transporting the children to the hospital because they were so seriously injured that they needed to be given blood transfusions while en route, according to the *Cumberland Evening Times*. Injured children were taken to Garrett Memorial Hospital, but the available beds there were quickly filled. Children were also sent to Sacred Heart Hospital in Cumberland and Preston Memorial in Kingwood, W. Va.

Four children were reported to have died in the bus when it was struck while three others died at the hospital. Janet

Deem, 12; Nancy Deem, 15; Merle Harvey, 11; Nancy Harvey, 12; Richard Hinkle, 11; Lee Hoffman, 11; Shirley Lee, 12, all died in the accident.

Roy was scared, not only about what had happened to the bus, but he couldn't find his older sister, Frances. He feared that she was dead, but he later saw her at Garrett Memorial being unloaded from an ambulance.

Frances Dixon was among the 11 children who were seriously injured. She had a broken back, a broken collar bone, a broken cheek bone, and a torn Achilles tendon. She spent the next four months in a body cast, but she survived.

Garrett County School Superintendent Dr. Willard Hawkins wrote an article for the Oakland Rotary Club bulletin the week after the accident, and it was reprinted in *The Republican* on September 17.

He wrote, in part, "I had a very busy and I thought important schedule planned for last Thursday and Friday. I hurried to work on Thursday morning to get at these important things I had to do, only to receive a call a few minutes later that took me to the scene of the accident. How unimportant all of my important work soon became."

He praised all of the members of the community who had answered the call to help however they could during the crisis. He noted that Garrett County Hospital staff had been all hands on deck in their efforts to care for the injured children. Ministers from throughout the county were on hand to counsel the grieving, and the Maryland State Troopers helped manage all of the chaos that was going on that day.

You can learn more about the accident from the display at the Garrett County Transportation Museum.

Floods Nearly Sweep Away Kitzmiller

During the last week of March 1924, warm temperatures began melting the snow on the mountains. March 28 dawned with an overcast sky. The temperatures were warm, and a light rain fell throughout the day and into the night. Both the temperature and rain helped even more snow melt.

As residents along the North Branch Potomac watched the water rise, they realized there might be a problem. According to the 1926 Kitzmiller High School Yearbook, around 9 p.m., a night watch was posted on the river in case it overflowed its banks. At 2 a.m. in the morning of March 29, the night watch sounded the alarm. Similar alarms were sounded in communities all along the river.

People in Shallmar, Kitzmiller, and other communities threw on clothes, grabbed what they could and ran for higher ground. Lanterns flashed, swinging back and forth as people hurried out of their homes into the pitch dark of the night. Parents called to their children to try and keep them from getting separated in the darkness.

Soon enough, people heard the sound of rushing water where there shouldn't be any. As dawn broke, they could see chicken coops with chickens in them, debris, livestock and even houses rush by in the flooded streets of their towns. One house in the North Branch floated by with a light still burning in an upper window. It was only extinguished when the house smashed into the Kitzmiller bridge and became debris. The flood eventually swept away the bridge, too.

Samuel Beeman, his wife, Beeman's father and the Beemans' two children climbed onto a tall tree when the flood waters got too high in Kitzmiller and began filling their home, according to the *Cumberland Evening Times*. The raging river eventually washed away their house. The water pushed against the tree they were on while at the same time carrying away soil from around the roots. The tree uprooted and toppled into the river taking all the members of the Beeman family with it.

Another man was last seen wading on Main Street in Kitzmiller before he turned up missing and was presumed drowned. Other people lost livestock. The flood waters also took out the tipple at the nearby Pee Wee Mine and thirty loads of coal, roughly sixty tons, were washed into the river near the Potomac Manor Mine when the coal cars were tipped over by the floods.

The floodwaters began receding around 11 a.m., and people came down from the high ground to see what was left of their homes, according to the Kitzmiller High School Yearbook. Towns all along the North Branch Potomac felt its effect. Cumberland had $4 million in flood damage, according to Al Feldstein in his book *Feldstein's Postcard Views*. Closer to home, Chaffee, the next small coal-mining town downriver from Kitzmiller was so severely damaged from the flooding that it was abandoned and the miners moved to Vindex. In Kitzmiller and Shallmar, twenty-one houses plus some cars and trucks were either destroyed or washed away, according to the book *Ghost Town of the Upper Potomac*.

Even after the North Branch Potomac had returned to within its banks, some of the families whose homes were too damaged or washed away spent several nights sleeping in the

Shallmar power-house. It was large enough to house them all and high enough up the mountain that it hadn't flooded at all.

The cost of recovering from the 1924 flood contributed to the failure of the Wolf Den Coal Company in 1927 and its restructuring as the Shallmar Mining Company with the same officers.

The Morning Oakland Burned

R obert Shirer woke up from a deep sleep the morning of July 12, 1898, when the sound of a whistle and church bell wouldn't stop. When he opened his eyes, wondering what the reason for the noise was, he saw that his bed was on fire and some of his room. He jumped from his bed and ran out of the burning building with only his night clothes on. It was a narrow escape that left him with slight burns.

Outside, it appeared as if all of Oakland was on fire.

C. L. Haught, a clerk at the Oakland Pharmacy, had been the first person to see the fire that morning. Like Shirer, he had been asleep, but he came awake much earlier than usual because of unusual noises. He sat up when he realized that he had been "aroused from his sleep by a roaring and creaking noise under his window and a flare of light in his room," *The Republican* reported.

It was not yet 4 a.m. so it should have been dark and quiet outside. He walked to the window and saw that the saloon owned by James Reynolds had caught fire. The saloon abutted the building where his room was so it was only a matter of time before it caught fire, too.

Haught threw his pants and ran out into the street shouting, "Fire!"

Dr. Henry W. McComas was the first person to appear. He had been out of town for business reasons and had just arrived back at his office. More people soon roused, and someone started blowing the whistle at the electric light plant to sound the general alarm for Oakland. Another person rang to bell in the Lutheran Church to alert residents of the danger.

"This had the effect to arouse the whole town, and in a remarkably short time hundreds of people were at work vainly striving to check the rapidly advancing flames and in saving goods from the burning buildings and those which were in danger of burning," *The Republican* reported.

The roaring fire soon spread to the surrounding buildings – the *Mountain Democrat* Newspaper Building, the Offutt Building, and the Ravenscroft Building. Because of the parched conditions the area had been experiencing for the past month "these buildings burned like tinder and in a remarkably short time they were in ashes." The newspaper reported.

From the Offutt Building, the fire jumped to a two-story frame building at the rear of the Garrett County bank and then to a new building owned by D. E. Offutt on Railroad Street. This building housed the law office of W. A. Daily, a confectionary story, and a home.

From the Ravenscroft Building, the fire jumped to an adjoining building that housed a general store, seamstress shop, tailor's shop, jewelry store, and the home of Joseph Harned, who owned the general store.

"When the alarm sounded he and family were asleep and they had just time to escape from the building in the clothes they could grasp as they hurried from their rooms," *The Republican* reported.

Their youngest son had rushed outside dressed only in his night dress and wrapped in a blanket. Someone in the crowd saw the lone child and took him to a neighbor's house. His mother, who had been out of her mind with fright because she thought that he hadn't gotten out of the building, found him there later.

All of the buildings on the south side of 2nd Street burned completely. *The Republican* reported that "when it was seen none of them could be saved from the fire willing hands were turned to the north side of that thoroughfare in the hope that by keeping the flames from the store building owned and occupied by Messrs. J. M. Davis & Son as a hardware establishment the greater portion of the business and resident part of the town could be saved."

The still smoldering ruins of Oakland after the great fire of 1898. Photo courtesy of the Garrett County Historical Society.

The townspeople had formed a bucket brigade to try and fight the fire. The fire department had a chemical engine that was also being used to try and put out the fire. It was overwhelming, and Oakland Mayor R. S. Jamison telegraphed Mayor George A. Kean of Cumberland for help. Kean promised to send a fire company, but that help would be hours away.

Jamison's message may have been one of the last to get out of Oakland before the fire burned down three telegraph poles, taking the wire with it. A correspondent with the *Warren* (Pa.) *Democrat* had been transmitting a story to the newspaper when he had lost communications. The message read, "A fire started in the largest general store here, the flames spreading rapidly. Half the town is threatened, the street being blocked with poles burning." It had then ended unfinished.

Meanwhile, the group trying to stop the fire at the J. M. Davis & Son store was having a rough time.

"Here the fight centered for half an hour through smoke and flame, with arms and faces blistered from the intense heat, fighting against almost a forlorn hope, with increasing tension to the nerves but with no flagging or hanging backward, men and women, boys and girls, gave willing assistance and after the front of the Davis store had been burned through in a hundred places with broken glass falling and cinders hurtling through the air, men of bravery and with that determination of purpose which has always denoted the citizens of Oakland, the victory was won and thousands of dollars' worth of valuable property, and probably valuable lives, were saved," *The Republican* reported.

The bucket brigade was crucial in saving the Davis Building. When the chemical engine had run dry and needed to be refilled, the was only the work of the bucket brigade that had kept the fire from advancing.

The help from Cumberland arrived at 7:30 a.m. after the fire had been contained. Kean had called out the 25 men, an engine, and hose reel, and loaded them on a flat car with a passenger coach attached. The special B&O Railroad train left Cumberland at 6:05 a.m. When the train passed through Piedmont, a company of firefighters there boarded the train to help fight the fire.

When the firefighters arrived in Oakland, they set up their hoses to draw water from the Little Yough to douse the embers of what had been part of Oakland's business district. It took another three hours before the firefighters were satisfied that the fire was entirely out.

Communications outside of Oakland had been cut off for an hour until telegraph wire could be restrung. Regular trains along the B&O were delayed until the tracks were inspected to make sure that the fire hadn't damaged them.

In all, 16 businesses and buildings were damaged or lost in the fire. The initial damage report totaled more than 50,000 (about $2.5 million in today's dollars), and only $19,900 of it was covered by insurance.

The displaced businesses found other locations to operate from until new buildings could be built. Some rented a room at the Central Hotel to use as a business office. The hotel had been saved from damage in the fire by the large trees in front of it. Those trees had caught the embers sailing through the air that might have caught the hotel on fire. Benjamin Sincell allowed James Litzinger to operate his *Mountain Democrat* newspaper from *The Republican* offices until Litzinger could find a permanent office.

A Baltimore newspaper reported that an arsonist had set the fire. The investigation ruled that out as the cause but did not state what had caused the massive fire.

WHEN COAL WAS KING

The Champion Coal Miner of the World

W hen Lawrence B. Finzel trudged home from the coal mines each day, he knew he had done a good day's work. In fact, he knew he'd done a good two or three days work.

In 1917, Finzel was called the champion coal miner of the world "who just before the recent wage increase became effective earned $347.92 in one month mining coal," according to *The Republican.*

He accomplished this by mining an average of 12 tons of coal each day at a time when a good day's work at the region's mine was five tons of coal.

"He leaves his home with his fellow miners and returns with them and does as much work as two or three ordinary miners with apparent ease," the *Cumberland Evening Times.*

Though he accomplished this great feat in Hooversville, Pa., Finzel was born in Garrett County and had worked in mines in Maryland and West Virginia, performing similar feats.

He came from a mining family. His father, Henry, was a German immigrant who settled in Garrett County and mined for half a century. Finzel was one of six brothers who were taught to be industrious not only in the coal mines but on the family farm.

"When the farm was in good state of cultivation and the work could be done by the boys in the evening, the boys went into the mines. After digging coal the greater part of the day, they came home and worked on the farm," *The Republican* reported.

Miners got paid based on how much coal they mined each day, and Lawrence Finzel could dig more than twice as much coal as the average coal miner. Photo courtesy of *Whilbr.org*.

His industriousness paid off for him. Coal mining pays miners by the amount of coal they mine. When Finzel worked for the Consolidation Coal Company, he was "drawing the largest pay for any miner in the small-vein mines in that region," according to *The Republican.*

He took a job in West Virginia working for the Saxman Coal and Coke Company near Richwood. "Working in a seam of coal three feet high, he earned $2,360 in one year, and an average of $196 per month. He loaded 4,000 tons of coal, an average of 12 tons daily. This is believed to be the greatest amount of coal ever dug by one miner in the State of Virginia," *The Republican* reported.

He then moved his family to Hooversville to work for the Custer & Sanner Coal Company. He was told that the previous earnings record for a miner was $175 in two weeks. Finzel set to work to break the record. During the first two weeks of October 1917, he earned $136.97 (with a reduced car supply), and during the back end of the month, he earned $211.05, which broke the previous record handily. Finzel even thought he could have done $400 during the month if he had had a good car supply in the early part of the month.

It was such an accomplishment that it made news around the country, particularly in newspapers in coal-mining regions.

He also held a record for mining 600 tons of coal in a month, according to the *Cumberland Evening Times.*

"On one occasion he was given a heading to drive and two other miners were given an air course. In one month Finzel had driven the heading sixty feet deeper in the coal than the others had driven the air course," the Connersville, Ind., *Daily Examiner* reported.

For all his great accomplishments in the mine, Finzel was not a large man. He was described as being of medium height, and his friends called him "the little big digger." Because of his great feats, he was often examined by doctors looking for something that made him special. The *Cumberland Evening Times* noted that "a physical examination at John Hopkins Hospital he was pronounced the finest muscled man that ever came to the institution."

Finzel died two years later after his record-setting month, on January 19, 1919, from complications from pneumonia. He left behind a wife, a daughter, and three sons.

According to the *Charleston Gazette*, Finzel's headstone read: "He led the world in coal mining during the World war."

Tracking the Underground Pony Express

H erds of ponies once roamed Maryland, though most people rarely saw them. They were pit ponies whose job it was to haul the coal from Maryland's coal mines.

The first use of ponies in coal mines date back to 1750 when they were utilized in a mine in Durham, Great Britain.

In one instance, Ray O'Rourke wrote for the *Baltimore Sunday Sun Magazine*, "Twenty-odd ponies that haul coal from under some 2,000 acres of Maryland territory are never seen in this State, and never breathe the air over it."

These ponies hauled coal for the Stanley Coal Company in Crellin. Though the mine was under Maryland, the entrance was in nearby West Virginia. Miners had to walk from Crellin across the state line and then backtrack once they were in the mine.

The mine's location also created some political headaches with Maryland and West Virginia governments fighting for the tax revenue from the pit. Eventually, a compromise was reached where West Virginia inspected the mine while the miners paid Maryland income taxes and the Stanley Coal Company paid unemployment taxes to Maryland.

The ponies were stabled near the mine entrance in West Virginia, so that is where Okey Jenkins, the stable boss, lived. At any given time, he had about 20 ponies that he cared for. Jenkins was a large man weighing in at 305 pounds at age 63. Besides stable boss, he also functioned as the harness maker, veterinarian, pony trader and pony trainer for the mining company.

He worked out of a small two-foot by four-foot office with a sturdy swivel chair as its only furnishing. Harnesses, tools, and surgical instruments hung from hooks on the wall.

Jenkins lived close by in a small house that showed his affection for horses. A merry-go-round pony was mounted on its pole in his front yard, and pony bells served as his doorbell.

Mining ponies and mules were needed to haul the mined coal from the mines. Some rarely saw the light of day. Photo courtesy of the Albert and Angela Feldstein Collection.

He left for work each morning at 4 a.m., walking down the hill to his small office. By 5 a.m., he was at work feeding all of the ponies and by 6:40 a.m., he would be harnessing the ponies and leading them to the mine where they would haul coal cars from 7 a.m. to 2:30 p.m.

"Unlike ponies that are kept underground all their lives in deep-pit mines, the Crellin ponies never contract the blindness that constant darkness brings," O'Rourke wrote.

Despite keeping their sight, the ponies still worked more than 400 feet underground. Ponies were used because they could work in low, narrow spaces. This meant that the mine shafts didn't need to be as wide as they would have needed to be if small engines had been used to move the coal out of the mine.

A miner with a Shetland Pit Pony in the coal mine. Photo courtesy of *horseandman.com*.

The ponies worked hard in the mines. A 550-pound pony could pull a 2,200-pound coal car loaded with two tons of coal. Jenkins preferred ponies for this job because they didn't have to duck in the low-ceiling shafts as horses would have to do and their shorter height gave them a better angle to lean forward and pull the load. He was also partial to Welsh ponies for the work because he said they had greater stamina.

The ponies needed stamina, too. Besides having to pull such heavy loads, they might pull up to 50 such loads a day, though most days it less.

"They're like high-strung men. They feel their responsibility, and they show it," Jenkins said.

A pit boy with a pit pony in a coal mine in England. Photo courtesy of *horseandman.com*.

The ponies and Jenkins worked six days a week. When he was off on a buying trip for more ponies, an assistant would work his shift. However, Jenkins always made sure to check on the ponies when he returned.

"Should any of them ever show welts or whip mark, he says: 'Better watch-there's gonna be a fit throwed around here. We don't want these little fellas all boogered up,'" O'Rourke wrote.

Part of this care came because Jenkins truly loved his ponies, but he was also protecting the mine's investment. Jenkins could buy an untrained pony for $250, but once it was trained, it was worth $1,000. Keeping the ponies healthy also ensured many productive work years. A pony could start hauling coal at age three and continue until it was 25.

The last pit pony retired when the New Gladstone Mine in Centerville, Iowa, closed. The *New York Times* wrote in its review of the book, The Last Pony Mine, "With the closure of the New Gladstone Coal Mine, the practice came to an end. This program documents the life of pit ponies and the men who worked beside them. Mainly used for hauling coal to the surface, horses were eventually replaced by modern machinery. In their heyday, they were a special breed; built for the claustrophobic and tight fit of the mines. The pony drivers had to develop strong bonds with these animals to guarantee safe conditions. In the end, success depended on partnership."

Kitzmiller Takes a National Mine Safety Title

D ying in a cave-in is a fear of every miner. Yet, deep miners overcome their fear daily, knowing that should something happen, their fellow miners will do everything in their power to rescue them.

"Sparked by a tragedy which took the lives of five miners in November 1948 fellow employees and citizens [of the Kitzmiller area] began to train rescue units in the event of future emergencies," according to an article in *Tableland Trails.*

Most mining companies have similar teams of miners trained in rescue techniques. To encourage these teams of miners to think and act fast to evaluate problems and rescue trapped miners, a national competition was put together where coal rescue teams competed against each other.

Shallmar resident George Brady remembered watching the Kitzmiller mining rescue team train in wooden mine shafts that had been constructed in Shallmar, which was the next town up the Potomac River from Kitzmiller. Harry Buckley, the district mine inspector; L. C. Hutson of the University of Maryland and Fred Baker of the U.S. Bureau of Mines conducted the training exercises.

In 1951, the six best diggers were chosen to go to Columbus, Ohio, to compete in the National Mine Rescue and Safety Championships. It was the first national championship to be held in 20 years.

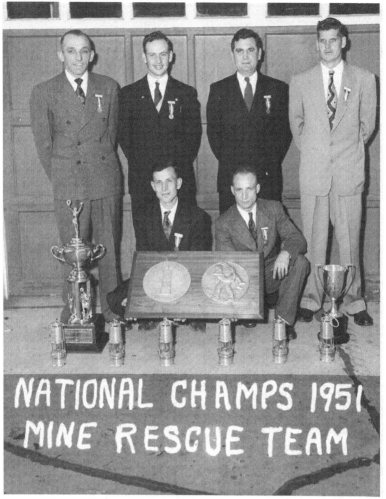

The Kitzmiller National Mine Safety Rescue Team was the best in the country in 1951. Photo courtesy of Robert Hartman.

The competition was held at the Ohio State Fairground on October 2, 1951. The Kitzmiller team was one of 15 teams from Ohio, Illinois, Kentucky, Maryland, Pennsylvania, and West Virginia competing for the national title among coal miners. The teams were sent into a constructed mine shaft to deal with a simulated mine disaster. The simulations included smoke, gas, fires, injured miners, and dead bodies.

It was a test of the miners' equipment, physical condition, and abilities. They solved hypothetical mine emergency problems and were judged on how well the teams used mine rescue procedures and how fast they solved the problems. They also had to show they could identify and fix rescue equipment and perform first aid on miners with simulated injuries.

At the end of the competition, the team from Kitzmiller walked away with the national title. The second place team was from the U.S. Steel, Coal Division, in Uniontown, Pa. The third place team was the Consolidation Coal Company of Kentucky from the Clover Split Mine.

Carl Schell, Chester Evans, Carl Paugh, Mervin Sims, Richard Sherwood and Lee Hartman were the members of the winning team. Schell, Evans, and Paugh were miners with the Garrett Coal Corp. Sims worked with the Pritt Brothers Coal Company. Sherwood was a digger for the Wolf Den Coal Corporation, and Hartman worked for the Sugar Coal Company. Each miner received a Congressional medallion from the U.S. Bureau of Mines as well at trophies.

"I was more than pleased with the outcome. The residents of Kitzmiller are to be complimented for having such an organized group in their community," said Frank Power, Director of the Maryland Bureau of Mines.

The following May, a civil defense center opened in Kitzmiller, and Maryland Governor Theodore McKeldin came to town not only for the opening but to also honor the national champion mine rescue team.

As part of his remarks, McKeldin noted that Kitzmiller's rescue team did not stop training once they became national champions. They continued their preparedness. "This group," he commented, "forms a hard core of trained personnel ready to go anywhere in the state or area if a disaster strikes, and stands out as an example to all other communities."

The team eventually disbanded when the mines in the area began closing.

Maryland's Second-Largest Mine Closes

B y 1950, the mining operations at Vindex were the second largest in Maryland, but that didn't save it from being shut down at the end of March.

"Last year, the Vindex deep mine and the Laurel Stripping Company nearby produced 107,908 tons of coal," *The Republican* reported in 1950.

That was less than half of what the mine had produced in 1947 (228,000 tons of coal) when it had led other Maryland mines in coal produced.

Andrew B. Crichton, of Johnstown and president of the Johnstown Coal and Coke Company, made the announcement saying, in part, that Manor Mine No. 3 and a nearby strip-mining operation were going to be closed because there was "no place to turn suddenly for a new coal mine."

Vindex opened in 1906 as the company town for miners of the Three Forks Coal Company. At its peak in the 1920s, Vindex had a school, church, company store, 75 homes, and 500 residents, Al Feldstein wrote in his book, *Garrett County*. The town was also served by the Chaffee extension of the Western Maryland Railway.

Stephen Schlosnagle added in his book, *Garrett County: A History of Maryland's Tableland*, that "During the peak years nearly all boasted town bands and baseball teams, churches, schools, and stores."

As the fortunes of coal companies ebbed, companies

closed and combined. Three Forks Coal Company sold the mine to the Chaffee Coal Company, which in turn later sold the mine to the A. B. Creighton Coal Company before being sold to its final owners, the Johnstown Coal Company.

Mrs. Harold Adams, the wife of the former superintendent of the Vindex mines and postmistress of the town, stands at the ruins of the old Vindex Post office.

"During World War II years, the company enjoyed a boom with a peak employment being 275 men both inside and outside the Vindex Mine," the *Cumberland News* reported. "The death knell was tolled on the deep mine operation in March 1950 when the company could not compete with stripped coal in the face of tough market conditions and high wage costs at the Vindex Mine." Some miners earned as much as $25 a day (around $343 in 2015 dollars).

The closure of the mine at Vindex on March 31, 1950, left 180 miners out of work.

It was another blow to the Maryland coal industry.

"Western Maryland's mine industry is slowly being squeezed out of operation, coal men familiar with the area fear," the (Uniontown) *Morning Herald* reported.

The Wolf Den Mine in Shallmar had shut down a year earlier. A month before Mine No. 42, the largest in Maryland had closed.

"Charles L. Briner, head of the Oakland branch of the Department of Employment Security, said there are no jobs for them in Garrett county," *The Republican* reported.

He was dealing with 3,000 out of work miners (about 15 percent of the county's population) with no work for them. Many other miners were working on reduced hours.

The ruins of the Vindex Company Store in 1991. Photo courtesy of the Albert and Angela Feldstein Collection.

The *Morning Herald* reported that the county had instituted its own welfare program that put out of work miners to work on improving county roads. The problem was that program was starting to run out of money and work for all of the miners.

Once the mine shut down, not everyone moved away. Many had nowhere to go. Pensioners, in particular, remained in their homes. Those who found jobs gradually moved away nearer where their new jobs were located.

The *Cumberland News* reported in 1967 that the last of these residents either died or moved away earlier that year. The 6,000 acres that comprised the mine and town was sold to James Polino of Elkins who planned on using it for strip mining and deep mining.

Today, what remains of Vindex makes it one of Garrett County's ghost towns.

Violence in the Tablelands

I n the early 20th century, gasoline and fuel oil began replacing coal as a source of heat. It also powered the horseless carriages that were growing in number across the country. Less demand meant less money paid for the coal. Coal company profits dropped and so the pressure to cut wages or employees or both increased.

Up until that time, the United Mine Workers union had been finding it hard to get a foothold in Maryland because work conditions were good, at least as far as mining work went. Those men who did join the union had to do so in secret, meeting in the woods far from the coal company's eyes and ears. Being a union member could cost a Maryland miner his job.

The UMW called a national strike on April 1, 1922. Though most of Maryland's miners were non-union, they walked out in support, including many of the miners in Garrett County. The miners were earning between $6.40 and $7.20 a day. The union was pushing for $7.50 a day.

In Maryland, the UMW used the strike to help promote its unionization effort for Maryland coal mines. Previous attempts to unionize Maryland miners had been made in 1879, 1882, 1886, 1894, and 1900.

Though Maryland diggers had issues with whatever mining company was running the mine, at times they also had reason to doubt the union's commitment to them. During the 1882 strike, the National Knights of Labor failed to financially support striking miners, which weakened the miners' ability to continue striking. County miners remembered this when the 1894 strike call came, and some miners refused to strike because they feared the union wouldn't financially back them.

Miners ride a coal car out of a mine. Photo courtesy of Western Maryland's Historical Library.

When the UMW national strike ended on August 15, the Garrett County miners stayed out in an effort to win union recognition. The UMW supported the strikers with money and a food commissary. The mining companies, for their part, brought in strikebreakers from Cleveland, Pittsburgh, and West Virginia. They were armed with automatic weapons and even machine guns.

Some of the conflicts were minor like the time that a young Kenny Bray built a snowman in his front yard that was holding a sign with the word "SCAB" written on it in large letters so that it could be easily read from his neighbor's house. The neighbor was a miner who had crossed the picket line and wasn't too happy to be called the slur for a non-striker.

"He cursed me and ran me into the house," miner Kenny Bray wrote in his unpublished memoirs. "My mother came out and ran him into his house."

You don't cross a coal miner's wife, especially one who is also a mother. It's like trying to hold a greased rattlesnake and just as deadly.

Miners enjoying lunch together. Photo courtesy of Western Maryland's Historical Library.

In one instance, union miners' wives planned to jump the non-union miners in one neighborhood. The women were armed with clubs and rotten eggs. One woman even had a bush with plenty of thorns on it that she planned on using as a painful switch. The women hid behind a building lying in wait for the miners.

The first miner came walking along. Bray wrote, "The women came out and began to beat him, one woman hit him across the head with the bush knocking his hat off. Another woman began to slash him across the rump with a pick handle when he stooped to pick up his hat. They hit him with only one egg. They were saving the other eggs for the next man."

The first man ran off to his house and the women laid in wait for the next man. However, the first miner returned to warn the unsuspecting miner. The first miner also had the women arrested for attacking him. During the trial, the miner showed the justice of the peace where he had been hit with the bush. One woman in the audience jumped up and told the miner to drop his pants and show where she had hit him with the pick handle.

Miner George Brady told about another incident during the strike in Kitzmiller. Union miners blocked the one-lane bridge across the North Branch Potomac between Kitzmiller and Blaine. They drove two cars toward each other from opposite ends of the bridge. When the cars met near the middle, no one could drive around them. The drivers got out of their cars and began yelling at each other for the other one to back up.

It was all a ruse. The performance had been staged to block the bridge at just the right time. A truck from one of the mines came rumbling down the road carrying supplies for the mine. It couldn't cross the blocked bridge, though. So the driver stopped the truck.

That was just what the union miners wanted. A group of them rushed from their hiding places and put boards with nails sticking out of them under the truck's tires so that the truck wouldn't be able to move without blowing all of its tires.

The driver was prepared for union violence. He pulled a shotgun off the rack behind his head and stuck it out the window and warned the miners to clear off.

That gave the miners pause since none of them wanting to

be shot. A woman from Shallmar ran up to the truck and jumped on the running board. She grabbed the barrel of the shotgun and placed it against her breast. Now she was a big, buxom lady, so she had plenty of breast to cover both barrels of that shotgun and then some.

Miners in Dodson relaxing. Photo courtesy of Western Maryland Historical Library.

"If you want to shoot someone, shoot me, you son of a bitch," the woman yelled.

The driver couldn't bring himself to shoot a woman, especially an unarmed one, though he might have been thinking about it. The important thing for the miners was that the driver hesitated. That gave the miners time to get the shotgun from him. It went flying into the river.

The miners then beat the holy hell out of the driver. He didn't die, but he spent some time in the hospital recovering from the beating he took.

Things just got worse. Striking miners in Western Maryland

would shoot at non-union miners who were still working. In the extreme instances, people were even murdered.

The UMW called off the nearly 20-month strike in November 1922 without unionizing the mines. What did happen was many miners lost their jobs not only because the mining companies were careful who they rehired, but because the strike crippled the mining industry in the area.

Whispers of Communities Gone

W ith the discovery of coal in 1899, Kitzmiller, nestled in a valley in Garrett County and alongside the Upper Potomac River, quickly grew into a boom town. It had a bank, bakery, hotel, post office, high school, doctors, dentist, movie theater, barber shops, gas station and more. Just before the Great Depression, the population was estimated at around 1,500 people.

Then the coal mines in the region began shutting down, and people moved on to find work. Many of the businesses closed because their customers had gone. Today, the population is about 300 people.

Kitzmiller is actually quite lucky. It still exists even if it is a shadow of former self. The people who remain work hard to make it a good place to live, though they do so without many of the amenities the town used to have.

Ghost towns

So many communities along the Upper Potomac are no longer. Some have left behind a few houses or a road to nowhere that has fallen into disrepair, but even more have been entirely swallowed up by the mountains.

Vindex had a company store that housed a post office and an open second floor that was used for recreational activities and theater productions. It had its own elementary school, though the high school students went to Kitzmiller. It also had 500 residents living in company-owned homes.

The children of Kempton, when the town was still a busy coal-mining town. It is now one of the ghost towns along the North Branch Potomac River. Photo courtesy of the Garrett County Historical Society.

Kempton began as a lumber town and continued life as a coal town. The company houses were built on a strip of land three-quarters of a mile long and a few hundred feet wide. Each house had four or six rooms with a front yard and a garden in the back. Kempton had a school, an opera house and a company store that had a lunchroom, bowling alley, dance floor, auditorium, and post office. A branch line of the Western Maryland Railway ran into the town.

Then the mines closed and, as happened with many of the company towns, the buildings were torn down to remove them from the tax rolls. In Kempton, thousands of dollars of company scrip were dumped down a mine shaft. The people moved on.

"They bought necessary commodities in company-owned

stores and used company-issued scrip currency. They depended socially and economically on the success of their companies, and when their companies suffered, they suffered," Stephen Schlosnagle wrote in *Garrett County: A History of Maryland's Tableland.*

Vindex, Kempton, Shallmar, Wallman and others are gone with only a name and a few houses remaining to recall the memories of the towns that once thrived.

"Most of these ghost towns can be identified, when one finally reaches their locations, by ruins of old buildings amid the brush, cement foundations of former bridges, other structures, and remains of coal tipples. The real tombstones, however, are the large gob piles, partially hidden by tangled brush and scrub trees on the hillsides, that mark the coal mines that once gave life to so many of these old towns," George Fizer wrote in *Ghost Towns of the Upper Potomac.*

When ghost towns thrived

The small coal and lumber towns along the Upper Potomac River were originally built to serve the needs of businesses in those remote areas. Houses were built for the employees. Because those employees were far from larger towns and cities (some could only be accessed by rail), businesses, schools, churches and post offices also needed to be built to provide for the needs of the employees. It was a symbiotic relationship between employee and business.

"When the timber and coal played out, the towns died—there was no longer a reason for their existence," said Dan Whetzel, a local historian interested in Western Maryland's mining region. "The rugged terrain and remoteness inhibited alternative reasons for the residents to remain there."

These small, isolated towns with populations anywhere from a couple hundred to 1,500 people tended to attract immigrants to work in the mines, mills, and forests. The towns could be very homogenous, attracting mainly immigrants from a particular country.

"I suspect this was because families tended to draw other family members from abroad. Each town, therefore, had unique populations," Whetzel said.

However, when the mine or the mill shut down, the workers moved on to other small towns.

An old company house, in poor condition but still occupied. Photo courtesy of the Garrett County Historical Society.

Union violence

On April 1, 1922, the United Mine Workers called a national strike. Many mines had low pay and poor working conditions, though miners in Western Maryland "were said to be generally satisfied with their wages and working conditions," according to Kathryn Harvey in *The Best-Dressed Miners.* However, she notes different companies were found to be underpaying their miners for the amount of coal they mined by using light scales.

The vacant Shallmar Company Store is just about all that is left of the coal town. Photo courtesy of the Albert and Angela Feldstein Collection.

The Knights of Labor, the American Miners' Association, Miners and Laborers' Protective and Benevolent Association and the United Mine Workers of America had all tried to unionize workers in the preceding years without much success. Garrett County miners walked out in support of the strike, which lasted until August 15.

The mining companies, for their part, brought in strikebreakers from Ohio, Pennsylvania, and West Virginia. Guards were armed with automatic weapons and even submachine guns.

The situation erupted in violence at various times. Dodson was one site along the Upper Potomac where miners and strikebreakers got into fights and fired shots at each other.

Luke, Md.

Luke, just over the Garrett County line in Allegany County, once had a 1,000 people living in it. Now with a population of around 63 people, it is one of the smallest municipalities in the state. The sole industry in the town is the NewPage paper mill, but the company has been struggling against foreign competition. This has lead to layoffs and furloughs. Others employees commute into town rather than live there.

Not that there are many places to live anymore. During the years when the plant was expanding, the company bought up properties to tear down the houses and grow.

The most recent blow to Luke's livelihood is the closure of the U.S. Post Office at the end of April 2009. The reason given is that the U.S. Postal Service is struggling to remain profitable by reducing expenses. The Luke post office had generated only $100 in the last quarter of 2008 and the first quarter of 2009 and only four of the 60 post office boxes were rented.

Will Luke become another Maryland ghost town? That's for the future to decide. The remaining residents certainly hope not, but the town's population is smaller than most of the ghost towns were at their peak, and the town budget is nearly entirely dependent on taxes paid by NewPage.

When Christmas Came to Shallmar

B etty Mae Maule was one of 60 students who attended the two-classroom Shallmar School in November
1949. When teaching principal J. Paul Andrick
asked Betty Mae to write a problem on the blackboard one
day, the 10-year-old girl stood up at her desk and promptly
fainted.

Betty Mae and her siblings hadn't eaten anything all day.
Their last meal had been the night before when the eight
people in the family shared a couple apples.

Betty Mae Maule

This is how bad things had gotten in
the little coal town on the North
Branch Potomac River. What had
once been the jewel of Western Maryland coal towns was dying.

Operating only 36 days in 1948,
the Wolf Den Coal Corporation,
which owned Shallmar, came into
1949 struggling in vain to stay open.
The mine shut down in March, having
operating only 12 days that year.

A town starving

Shallmar's houses had once been considered among the nicest homes for miners in the region. Now they needed a fresh coat of paint and more than a few were boarded up because they were no longer livable or needed.

Shallmar's houses from the back in the 1940s as the town started to enter its decline. Photo courtesy of Robert Hanlin.

The Maule family had six children. When Andrick explained to Walter Maule and his wife, Catherine, that he knew their children hadn't eaten that day, Catherine's explanation was simple: The mine had closed.

Miners had collected unemployment, but it hadn't been much because the miners hadn't worked much in recent years. Even that meager amount had stopped in August.

Albert Males, chairman of the United Mine Workers local relief committee, had then used the union treasury to issue small relief checks of $2 to $7 a week to families. He only had $1,000 to split among four dozen families, so it hadn't lasted long.

The Maules had been eating only apples that the children had found on the ground at a nearby orchard. Those had run out the day before, which is why the family hadn't eaten that morning. It wasn't the first time they had gone without breakfast lately either.

"My children have forgotten what milk tastes like," Catherine later told a reporter for the *Cumberland Evening Times.* They hadn't had any meat or milk for four months.

Catherine assured Paul that they had managed to find enough cabbage and potatoes to get them through the next day. She was proud of this because, "We sometimes don't even have potatoes and cabbage," she said.

With the mine closed, there were no jobs in Shallmar. Only three people in town had cars and families couldn't afford the move.

J. Paul Andrick

Taking action

That night, Andrick started writing letters to anyone he could think of who might be able to help from the board of education to his U.S. senators. He also wrote to *The Republican* hoping to let people know about Shallmar's plight.

The next morning, Andrick had his wife make extra sandwiches for his lunch. He gave the sandwiches to the students he saw with nothing to eat at lunchtime, according to his son, Jerry. He not only gave the extra sandwiches away but his own lunch as well.

The men in Shallmar had tried to feed their families. They hunted each day but came home empty handed. Many deer in Western Maryland were dying from a disease in 1949 that reduced their numbers. Shallmar hunters only managed to bag four deer. The meat was appreciated, though.

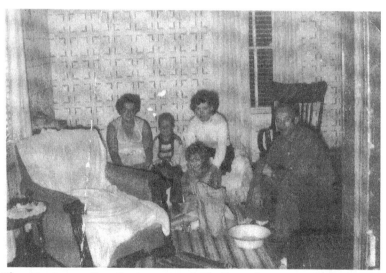

The Hartman Family in one of Shallmar's company houses, which shows how small the rooms were. Photo courtesy of Robert Hartman.

"I never cared much for venison, but it was the first fresh

meat in this house for three months," one woman told a reporter with the *Portland Sunday Telegram and Sunday Press Herald.*

John Crouse was one of the lucky hunters who bagged a deer in season, but it wasn't enough to keep his family of six children fed for too long. The Crouse family ate one meal a day, and on many days, that meal was potatoes and baked beans.

"It was the first time we had fresh meat in eight months," John's wife, Dolly, told *The* (Baltimore) *Sun.*

Word gets out

On December 8, 1949, residents picked up The *Republican* to read: "Shallmar Residents Are Near Starvation, Urgent Appeal Made For Food, Clothing and Cash." It was a front page story under the masthead of the newspaper.

Mine closings and poverty were nothing new to the region, but the fact that it was so bad that children were fainting from lack of food and others not able to attend school because they didn't have warm clothing was more than anyone with a conscience could handle.

Charles Briner, the Garrett County director of employment security for Maryland, was inundated with telephone calls that spanned the gamut from pleas for him to do something to help Shallmar to accusations that he was killing the miners.

The Oakland American Legion Auxiliary was quick to announce that it was starting a collection of clothes and food.

A *Cumberland Evening Times* reporter arrived in Shallmar on the day *The Republican* article came out. He interviewed residents for his own article, which ran the following day.

As Shallmar's story spread, more and more letters filled Paul's mail slot at the company store until finally all Paul was getting was a note from the postmaster and store manager, Baxter Kimble, saying to ask him for the mail.

The other person who started getting calls and letters was mine superintendent Howard Marshall. Reporters tracked him down in a Cumberland hospital recovering from minor surgery.

Students from the Shallmar School help unload some of the first items that arrived to help the town. Photo courtesy of the author's collection.

Marshall told reporters that he didn't know when the mine would reopen. He seemed to have little sympathy for the plight of his miners and their families.

"I ain't seen anyone starving yet," Howard told the reporters. His solution was that the county welfare system should take care of them. "They pay enough taxes," he said.

However, he wasn't entirely unsympathetic. The company wasn't trying to collect on its house rent or company store accounts. While the rent for the largest houses in town was only $12.60 a month, in some cases, rent hadn't been paid for over a year.

Help begins

A few days after the *Cumberland Evening Times* ap-

peared, a large truck rolled into town filled with fresh vege-
tables, meat packed on ice, canned goods, milk, dresses,
pants, and shirts. So many people had been calling the newspaper office asking where they could make donations that
newspaper collected donations and used a company truck to
make the delivery.

Seven-year-old sandy-haired Bob Hartman's eyes bugged
out at all the food. Then he saw a set of new Levi overalls
that looked like they would fit someone his size.

He told one of the men, "I'd sure like to have them
overalls."

The truck driver looked at Bob and his threadbare
clothes. "We'll see if we can't get them for you."

The man walked away. When he came back a minute later, he had the overalls in his arms and handed them to Bob.
He ran home and tried them on, pulling the stiff material over
his worn pants and shirt. The overalls weren't a perfect fit,
but it was good enough. He felt warmer without any drafts
whipping through the holes in his pants. Though Christmas
was still two weeks away, Bob felt like it was already
Christmas morning.

It looked like Christmas had come early to the town. Un-
shaven miners smiled behind their whiskers, mothers and
wives laughed as children grabbed at the clothing separated
into piles on tables in the union hall. Finding something they
liked, many children hurried home to try on the clothes. Others couldn't wait that long and began pulling on sweaters
over their summer shirts and trying on shoes. It was the first
time in weeks that some of them had been warm. Each family
also got enough food to last them a week.

With the town's sudden abundance, Andrick called for a
community meeting in the school to decide how to distribute
the food. He also told the gathered crowd that more would be

coming. The townspeople formed the Shallmar Relief Committee with Andrick as the chairman.

Relief efforts for the town got a big boost when CBS broadcaster Edward R. Murrow saw the story on the news wires and told the country about Shallmar on his Dec. 13 broadcast. More reporters, including Murray Kempton from the New York Post, started arriving in town to follow-up on the story of the town on the verge of starvation.

Students at Shallmar School get their first full meal in weeks as the school's hot lunch program begins. Photo from the author's collection.

Hot meals

By the time *The Republican* article had come out, the Garrett County Commissioners had already decided to fund a hot lunch program for Shallmar School, a building without a kitchen or cafeteria.

The union hall in the school could be used as the dining

hall, but there was no way to prepare the meals. The commissioners weren't willing to pay for a school expansion, and the kitchens in the houses in Shallmar were too small to make hot lunches for large groups. The solution was to cook the meals at Kitzmiller School, which was two miles away. The food was then dished out on plates that were covered and driven to Shallmar to be served while they were still hot.

With a plan in place, the commissioners allocated $1,200 to feed the students at Shallmar through the end of the school year. Andrick also spent money that the town had been receiving to pay for the students' portion of their lunches.

On Dec. 17, students sat down at two long wooden tables and had their first hot lunch in weeks, if not months.

Continuing aid

Trucks began arriving daily, braving the steep, narrow roads to reach Shallmar. A Baltimore meatpacking company sent a load of fresh beef. The Maryland Jewish War Veterans collected toys. The Amici Corporation in Baltimore sent $50 to the Oakland Chamber of Commerce to purchase candy for the children of Shallmar. Plus, Amici employees raised another $1,000 for the town in general.

The Baltimore American Legion collected so much food and clothing that it filled a room at the War Memorial Building. Among the donated items were 300 pounds of bacon, 250 loaves of bread, 200 quarts of milk, cases upon cases of canned goods and groceries, 100 pairs of shoes, 20 men's overcoats, 12 women's fur coats and blankets, not to mention toys for the children.

From New York City, the Save the Children Federation said that it would be sending toys and other needed things to the town. The Cumberland local of the United Brewery Workers of America also began raised money. Cumberland dairies donated milk and bakeries donated bread.

Shallmar even made international news when the *London Times* interviewed Andrick for a story. Letters arrived from other European cities like Paris with words of concern for Shallmar's residents.

A photographer took a shot of two-year-old Jean Ann Crosco sitting amid a pile of shoes being distributed. She was crying because none of them fit her. Numerous newspapers all around the world ran the picture and donations poured in specifically for Jean Ann. About a week after the photo was published, Jean Ann's mother told *The Iola Register*, "We have heard from every state in just a week. The kind people sent her dresses and other pretties. And she had about $200 in money gifts. And Jean Ann has forty—yes, forty—pairs of shoes."

The picture spurred A. K. Rieger, president of Gunther Brewing Company in Baltimore, to buy all of the children in Shallmar a new pair of shoes.

On December 21, the senior class at a Cumberland Catholic girls' school, canceled its own Christmas party to throw one for the children of Shallmar in the school. Two days later, the United Paper Workers Union Local 67 came to town to throw the children another party.

The Cumberland Optimist Club alone had delivered more than 15 tons of food and clothing to the town by the middle of December, and it was only one organization of dozens that delivered food.

As Christmas Day approached, the downstairs of the Andrick home filled with boxes and bags of letters and postcards; most of them with cash and checks in them. On the Friday before Christmas, 2,000 pounds of mail arrived in Shallmar.

Shallmar helps out

A week before Christmas, the Shallmar Relief Committee decided that since the town's residents had been blessed by so much kindness that they would be just as generous. The committee sent out food and clothing to help another 70 families in the region who were in just as bad a shape as families in Shallmar had been. Some got money, some got clothing, and they all got food.

"Today with $5,000 on deposit to their credit in a nearby bank, with tons of canned food piled up in their schoolhouse and more toys for their children than they know what to do with, the people of Shallmar have a realization of the Christmas message of "good will to men," George Kennedy wrote in *The Washington Star*.

On the Friday before Christmas, the members of the Shallmar Relief Committee filled the school classrooms with the items that had been held back from distribution. Children were allowed into the school to select one toy, one novelty, and one book. They were stunned at the abundance that confronted them and were hesitant to pick anything up. The girls, especially, were slow in selecting their dolls. They would look at the dolls without touching them, and once their decision was made, they would pick up their doll and hug it.

Of all of the children who came to the toy shop that day, only one returned. Six-year-old Elaine Paugh came back about an hour after she had finished her selections. She quietly told Andrick that her mother had told her to return the very nice doll that she had selected for herself. She was obviously fighting back tears as she handed the doll to Andrick.

Andrick told her to go ahead and select another doll, but he knew something that Elaine didn't. Her mother had picked out a beautiful doll for her on Friday evening and thought that another little girl should get the sweet doll that Elaine had picked out. Elaine would be sad for only a day.

Christmas in Shallmar. Photo courtesy of Jerry Andrick.

That evening, Paul dressed up as Santa Claus and delivered bags of candy, nuts, and oranges to each of the families in Shallmar.

Charlotte Crouse and her brother were fighting that evening and too excited about the coming of Christmas to go to

125

bed. Her mother finally had enough and told them, "If you don't stop fighting, Santa Claus won't come."

At that moment, Charlotte looked up and saw Andrick outside the window in the living room. Of course, she thought she was seeing Santa Claus. She quickly stopped fighting with her brother and was on her best behavior for the rest of the night.

The next morning Charlotte got the doll for Christmas that her parents had picked out for her.

At Christmas morning church services, preachers announced that children from surrounding towns would be welcome to come and pick out their own toys at the Shallmar School. The relief committee had decided that it wanted to make sure that all of the gifts were shared with other children who might not have a Christmas otherwise.

Donations to Shallmar and its residents continued flowing into town even after Christmas. With hunger only temporarily eased by what grew to an estimated $7,000 in cash and $30,000 in food, toys, clothing and other items by early 1950, Andrick and the Shallmar Relief Committee turned their attention to long-term solutions for the town's problems. The money lasted until the account was closed in May 1952.

THE WAR BETWEEN THE STATES

When the Confederates Raided Oakland

S unday morning, April 26, 1863, was a beautiful spring morning in Oakland. For the Union detachment of 57 enlisted men and two officers stationed in town to guard the Baltimore and Ohio Railroad, it was another day in paradise. No one was shooting at them. They weren't living in squalid conditions or eating field rations. The citizens of Oakland had welcomed them as guests.

And the young ladies! Well, they loved a man in uniform.

While many of the soldiers spent the morning accompanying their sweethearts to church, Private Cornelius Johnson with the Sixth West Virginia Infantry had picket duty along the southern road leading into Oakland about a mile south of town. It was a lonely job, especially when he thought of his friends with the pretty girls in town.

Then he saw a large group of mounted Confederate soldiers riding towards town, and he began to wish that he was lonely.

"He was scared, but scared or not he had a duty to perform before his trembling legs got him away from there," Ruth and Iret Ashby wrote in *The Glades Star*. "He must warn the soldiers in Oakland that something was wrong. He raised his gun and fired a warning shot over the heads of the approaching riders before taking to his heels across the nearby field, towards the shelter of the woods."

One of the Confederate soldiers chased him and shot at

him knocking the heel off one of his boots. The Confederate soldier captured Johnson and then rejoined the group heading toward Oakland.

"Not until they were in Oakland did he learn why he had heard no gunfire," the Ashby wrote. "The raid had been carried out so quickly that his comrades had had no chance to rally against such overpowering numbers."

An estimated 800 Confederate cavalrymen commanded by Col. Asher Harman of the 12th Virginia Cavalry rode into Oakland around 11 a.m. The soldiers moved quickly to capture the Union detachment.

Many of the soldiers were still attending church services and were arrested as they left church. While the Union soldiers seemed resigned to their arrest, their sweethearts weren't so willing to let their men go.

One Confederate soldier approached a Union soldier to arrest him. He tipped his hat to the girl accompanying the Yankee and informed the soldier that he was under arrest. The woman berated the Rebel, beginning with, "You baldheaded son of a ..."

When the Rebel returned with his prisoners, he said, "Please God, I never heard a woman talk that way before."

Southern sympathizers had apparently told Capt. John McNeill, who led a company of Rangers, that an officer was recovering from battle wounds at the Glades Hotel. A group of Confederates demanded that the hotel owner turn over the officer.

"To enforce their demand, they parked a small cannon on the railroad's Second Street crossing," John Grant wrote in *150 Years of Oakland*. "The owner denied that a Union officer was in the hotel, so the soldiers fired a shot down the railroad tracks."

It was a warning shot because the Rebels then turned the

cannon to face toward the hotel. The owner insisted that there was no soldier inside, and he invited the Confederates into the hotel to inspect it themselves.

"Legend says that the soldiers abruptly ended their search when they reached the hotel's bar," Grant wrote.

While the citizens weren't molested, generally, the Confederates did seize food and horses for themselves.

The raid was a smaller part of a larger Confederate action meant to disrupt the newly formed West Virginia government. The action involved 7,000 men split between Brig. Gen. William (Grumble) Jones and Gen. John Imboden. Harman's men were part of Gen. Jones's command. They were to follow the Northwestern Turnpike and move north through Moorefield, W. Va., and Petersburg, W. Va., burn the bridges at Oakland and Rowlesburg, W. Va., and destroy the railroad trestle over the Cheat River. Then they would join with Gen. Imboden at Buckhannon, W. Va.

The night before the Oakland raid, Gen. Jones's men had fought Union troops in Greenland Gap in Grant County and forced them to surrender. Col. Harman's men had then traveled through the night and reached Oakland before word of the previous day's fighting reached the town, which is one of the reasons the Union troops had been caught off guard.

The Rebels had seized the railroad station and cut the telegraph lines. Another group of men burned the No. 88 railroad bridge over the Youghiogheny River. A group of cavalrymen captured a freight train in Altamont, W. Va., uncoupled the engine and sent it west in the direction of the Youghiogheny River. The Rebels thought the bridge would be destroyed by then and the engine would topple into the river. However, because there was no engineer aboard, the boiler overflowed, and the engine stopped before it reached the river.

Meanwhile, in Oakland, the Union weapons were

destroyed, and the Yankees were paroled. Then the Confederate infantry left town heading toward what is now Terra Alta, W. Va.

The raid, while successful, had only a minimal impact. The No. 88 bridge was rebuilt within five days. Some of the other bridges, including the one over the Cheat River, weren't destroyed.

Gen. Jones summarized his action for Gen. Robert E. Lee, wrote, "In thirty days we marched nearly 700 miles; we killed from 25 to 30 of the enemy; wounded probably three times as man; captured nearly 700 prisoners, 2 trains of cars; burned 16 railroad bridges and one tunnel, 150,000 barrels of oil, many engines and a large number of boats, tanks, and barrels; bringing home with us about 1,000 cattle and probably 1,200 horses. Our entire loss was ten killed and 42 wounded; the missing not exceeding fifteen.

"My orders were in all cases to respect private property, irrespective of the politics and part taker, in the war by owners. Horses and supplies were to be taken indiscriminately. One or two stores were plundered."

While inconvenienced, the government of West Virginia did not waver, however.

McNeill's Rangers Try to Destroy Bloomington Bridge

C harles Hambright spent his days hawking newspapers on the trains that traveled between Cumberland and Grafton, W. Va. daily. Each trip of roughly 100 miles took about four hours, of which he had sold what newspapers he could well before the halfway point.

He was riding the morning train east on May 6, 1864, when it stopped unexpectedly in Bloomington, just across the North Branch Potomac River from Luke and Piedmont, W. Va.

"There were a number of McNeill's Rangers lined up on both sides of our train," Hambright wrote years later. "Each one of them had a revolver in each hand. We had a few Union soldiers on our train, all asleep. No shots were fired."

Capt. John McNeill had organized his men as Partisan Rangers under the authority of the Confederate Congress in 1862. They cooperated with the Confederate Army but operated independently. McNeill had 210 men under his command, though no more than two-thirds were ever together at once. McNeill and his men ranged throughout the Potomac Valley raiding Union outposts and supply trains and disrupting operations of the Union Army. They were efficient at their work.

The Rangers attacked a Union supply train of 80 wagons nearly Burlington, W. Va., on November 16, 1863. The Rebels captured 20 men and 245 horses and set the wagons on fire.

"Captain McNeill took to the mountains, and by a

wonderful march (for rapidity) escaped, though pursued by over six hundred men," Confederate General John Imboden wrote of the incident. McNeill lost only one man and had five wounded.

In 1864, the Rangers captured Romney, W. Va., and held it for three days, according to *History of Hampshire County.*

"One expedition after another was sent out by General [Benjamin] Kelley, the Union commander in his front, for the purpose of crushing him; and in giving orders to his subordinate officers the injunction was invariably repeated to 'Kill, capture, or drive McNeill out of the country!'" Ranger John Fay wrote about life with McNeill.

On this occasion, McNeill's Rangers had been given the job of burning the B&O Railroad machine shops in Piedmont and destroying the railroad bridge at Bloomington. It was yet another attempt by the Confederate Army to cut off the major east-west transportation route for the Union Army.

McNeill and 61 of his Rangers left Hardy County, W. Va., on May 3, arriving at Bloomington at daybreak, a time when McNeill favored attacking his targets.

"Scarcely had they reached the Baltimore and Ohio railroad at Bloomington when a train loaded with horses was passing," Leonora Wood wrote in the *Piedmont Herald.* "Captain McNeill ordered it stopped, but the engineer threw open the throttle and ran through at full speed. The Captain of the Rangers was not accustomed to having his orders disobeyed and was furious at seeing this prize escape."

The next train was eastbound, and it was successfully stopped. The engine was detached and three Rangers road it into Piedmont under a flag of truce. They demanded the surrender of the soldiers in the town.

Meanwhile, other Rangers cut the telegraph wires to prevent a warning being sent out. They hadn't been fast enough, though. A telegraph operator got off two quick messages – one to New Creek five miles away where there were thousands of Union soldiers stationed and one to Oakland where a train full of troops was preparing to head east.

17 Mile Grade, Allegheny Mountains, near Mountain Lake Park, Md.

A train crossing the old B&O railroad bridge at Bloomington that McNeill's Rangers tried and failed to destroy in 1864. Photo courtesy of the Albert and Angela Feldstein Collection.

Captain John Peerce and his small detail stopped two additional freight trains, Peerce gave out the food the trains were carrying to the citizens. Wood believed that this generosity resulted in one of the citizens warning the Rangers that the next train from the east would have soldiers aboard.

Peerce was skeptical, but he deployed men along the rail line to be ready for the next train. With Federal troops to the east and west of them and mountains to the north and south of them, the situation began to look bleak.

Peerce said, "I do not profess to having any of that kind of bravery which would endanger my own life and the lives of those associated with me, but I knew that McNeill's only chance lay in my charging that train, and capturing those soldiers before they could be informed as to our numbers."

His 10 men stopped the train and demanded the soldiers' surrender, which they did because they had no ammunition in their weapons. Peerce ordered the troops to detrain and leave their guns inside. Even facing unarmed soldiers, the Rangers were in a dangerous situation. There were 10 of them surrounding the train and about 100 soldiers, more than enough to overwhelm the Rangers if they chose to. So the Rangers bluffed and pretended as if a much larger force surrounded the train.

The rear cars of the train were filled mostly with civilians like Hambright. He and the others were ordered to detrain. They were sent on foot across the bridge into Piedmont while the Rangers set the train on fire.

"After we were released and were on the track, on our way to Piedmont just about opposite the Hampshire dump (where coal was dumped into cars), we saw Mulligan's Jackass Battery going up Westernport Hill, on the Maryland side of the river. They opened fire on the Rangers who had started up the hill on the West Virginia side of the river," Hambright wrote.

The Rangers retreated under the battery fire, but although they were in the open for more than a mile, no one was killed or wounded, and they successfully made their escape having only partially achieved their objective.

The citizens of Piedmont didn't fare as well as McNeill's Rangers. "But citizens of Hampshire Hill, the most thickly settled residential section of Piedmont, were in the direct line of battle, and several were killed and injured, among them a young lady and three children," Wood wrote.

A bird's eye view of Piedmont, W. Va. from early in the 20th century. Photo courtesy of the Albert and Angela Feldstein collection.

In another instance, cannon fire hit a house near the top of the hill where the Walsh Family lived. A four-year-old girl was killed, and her 19-month-old brother lost his arm. The boy, John T. Walsh, survived and went on to become a teacher in Allegany County for 48 years.

Hambright had his own secret that he was hiding from the Union soldiers. One of the Rangers in the raid was John Lynn of Cumberland. According to Hambright, when Lynn saw him on the train, the Ranger gave him some mail to pass along to Hambright's aunt in Cumberland. She was either a Confederate sympathizer or at least willing to make sure that mail from the Cumberland men who were part of McNeill's Rangers made its way to their families.

Garrett County Civil War Forts

W estern Maryland's Civil War forts made Fort Cumberland from more than 100 years earlier look like a palace. Fort Pendleton and Fort Alice were both located in Garrett County, though at the time it was still part of Allegany County.

The Confederate Army had started the construction of Fort Pendleton near Gorman in June 1861. It was named for Confederate Gen. William Pendleton who served as Gen. Robert E. Lee's chief of artillery. Another story has the fort being named for Philip Pendelton who owned the land on which it was built.

However, the Confederates abandoned the fort in July 1861 without a shot ever having been fired.

The 4th Ohio Infantry took over the unfinished fort in August and finished in by mid-September. "They cut timber between the hilltop fort and the river below; they dug trenches and built earthworks for nearly a mile down the hill and over its eastern slopes," according to Stephen Schlosnagle in his book, *Garrett County: A History of Maryland's Tableland.*

The fort was a seven-sided breastwork with a headquarters in other buildings inside. Outside of the breastworks were 5,000 feet of trenches that were covered with logs and planks.

The Union Army used the fort to guard the approach to the old Northwest Turnpike bridge and stayed there until January of 1862.

The soldiers' service there was not distinguished. Schlosnagle wrote that Gen. Benjamin Kelley noted that "the troops of Fort Pendleton were prone to neglect picket duty, avoid blockading road, and preferred fishing to military service." The men also tore the wooden siding from a nearby church and used it for firewood.

Kelley told the commander, Capt. Joseph M. Goodwin that he would be dismissed from the military if he didn't control his men. Goodwin didn't, but Kelley never carried through on his threat, probably because everyone involved knew that the fort had no strategic value and it didn't really matter what the soldiers were doing. "Strategically, the structure was an almost total waste of time and money during the period that it was garrisoned," Schlosnagle wrote.

The second Garrett County fort had a purpose, but it was too small to adequately fulfill that purpose when it mattered.

Oakland resident and Civil War enthusiast John Rathger worked with the Garrett County Historical Society to develop a trail to the Fort Alice and put together a sesquicentennial event that includes the fort and the Confederate raid on Oakland. He said at the time of the 1863 raid on Oakland, Fort Alice was pretty much just rifle pits near the B & O Railroad bridge over the Savage River. A blockhouse was added to the site later.

The test of the fort's defensive capability took place on April 26, 1863, when about 1,000 Confederate troops captured Oakland and the fort after firing only two shots.

"The first shot was from a sentry firing a warning shot for the people in Oakland, but nobody heard it because they were in church," Rathger said. "The second shot was fired at the sentry as the Confederate troops chased him. The shot took off his heel."

Confederate Gen. William Jones commanded the troops that included some of McNeill's Rangers and the 2nd Maryland Confederate Infantry unit.

"They had local men with them who knew the roads and territory who could help them through the area," Rathger said.

Oakland wasn't the Confederate target. They were heading toward Morgantown and Oakland was a target of opportunity. The Confederate troops arrested the Union soldiers stationed at the fort, burned the fort and the B & O bridge that the fort had been built to defend. The first group of Confederate troops came into Oakland at 11 a.m. and moved out by 3 p.m. Another group came through an hour later and passed through.

Schilling in the Service

E ven after the Union's poor start in the Civil War, Edward Schilling still felt it was his patriotic duty to enlist in the army. His parents felt differently, though.

Schilling wrote in his journal, "my dear parents would not hear of my going, therefore would not give their consent."

He persisted and told them that it was likely he would be drafted and forced to leave the family farm three miles west of Frostburg. Only then did his parents relent and consent.

"With feelings of pain and pleasure, I left home," Schilling wrote. "Pain, to leave my beloved father and mother, whom I might never see again on earth, and who had been so kind to me. Pleasure, in bright anticipation for the future, of I knew not what glory and renown."

On August 11, 1862, Schilling took the train from Cumberland to Baltimore where he enlisted in the Fourth Regiment, Maryland Volunteer Infantry, Company F. In these early days of his enlistment, Schilling was very much the country boy out of place in the big city. He enjoyed sightseeing as much as possible and marveled at something as simple as his train ride to Baltimore.

His first bit of action was at the beginning of September 1862 when his company was sent to Westminster to arrest secessionists. While the soldiers in his company were standing at attention, an unknown person fired a shot at the group. No one was hit, but the soldiers sprang into action. The company pickets fired shots back, but likewise, didn't hit anyone. It was enough to keep Schilling from sleeping that night.

The following day, his company arrested a dozen people who were identified by Union loyalists as secessionists and a deserter from the Seventh Maryland Infantry.

On September 18, the company board a train that took them up to Harrisburg, Pa., and then back into Maryland to Hagerstown. It was here where Schilling and the other soldiers first heard about the Battle of Antietam, which had happened a short distance to the south on the same day that they had left Baltimore.

On September 20, the soldiers marched out of Hagerstown not to help the wounded who were still strewn across the battlefield in Sharpsburg but to Williamsport.

Having been in the military about two months, Schilling wrote his parents on October 7 that "soldiering agrees with me when I first enlisted I weighed 125 pounds yesterday I weighed myself at the quartermasters and weighed 135 so in 8 weeks I have gained 10 pounds. I feel stout and hearty and lazy the boys all say that they never saw a person get thicker in the face than I have."

His diet consisted primarily of black coffee, salt horse (beef), shingles (crackers), fat bacon, pickled pork, beans, and potatoes.

His battalion stayed primarily in Williamsport, although it moved out for excursions to other places, often chasing after rumors of rebel companies moving through the area.

In one letter, he described his typical day. In the morning, he fell into formation for roll call and then had breakfast. From 9:30 a.m. to 11:30 a.m., he drilled with his company. Then came mail call. Then lunch. The second drills of the day ran from 3:30 p.m. to 5 p.m. and the soldiers marched in a dress parade until sundown. They then ate dinner by candlelight. A few times a week, he would attend services. Roll call again at 8 p.m. and lights out at 8:30 p.m. It was done at a leisurely pace with time in between to do whatever the soldier wanted.

On November 2, they marched east from Williamsport, over South Mountain and into Frederick. "On top of this mountain one of the Co F boys found a skull the remains of some poor soldier occasionally a piece of shell," he wrote.

In all, it was a 28-mile hike that they did in 15 hours. Schilling felt that they had made pretty good time given that they had to march laden down with equipment. In Frederick, the soldiers rode the train to Baltimore. They set up camp at the Cattle Show Grounds and settled down to idleness again.

Their primary duty was to guard newly drafted militia recruits. Schilling notes that about half of the recruits were substitutes who were paid up to $500 to enlist in someone else's place. "These substitutes sometimes bribe the guards to let them out and get away, but one was shot by running the blockade (as we call it) by some of our Co.," Schilling wrote.

His own pay was sometimes slow in coming, but when it did, he made sure to send some home to help his family.

His service continued through the war, and he was at Appomattox Court House to witness Gen. Robert E. Lee's surrender and the end of the Civil War. Following his discharge from the army in the summer of 1865, Schilling once again went sightseeing and took a tour of Washington, D.C. before heading home to Garrett County, or what would be Garrett County in 1872.

Following the war, Schilling became a master carpenter and moved to Cumberland. He would also become a businessman, sell insurance, and sell real estate.

He died in 1918 and is buried in Rose Hill Cemetery in Cumberland.

Who is "Genl. Scofield"?

A s the country remembers the men who fought in the Civil War more than a century ago, a general lies forgotten in a grave atop Meadow Mountain just off of old U.S. Route 40. The only clue to who this man was is a grave marker that answers few questions and raises more.

IN MEMORY OF
GENL. SCOFIELD
CIVIL WAR VETERAN
KILLED ON THIS MOUNTAIN
1894
Donated by
A.J. IRWIN & SON

For years, Marie Lancaster of Addison, Pa., cared for the grave making sure the grave was trimmed and occasionally bringing flowers or a U.S. flag to leave by the marker.

"We just saw the grave while we were taking a Sunday drive and, after looking at it up close, my husband and I were of the opinion that a high-ranking military man like Gen. Scofield deserved a more prominent burial place than an isolated spot on the side of a mountain," Lancaster said in a 1992 interview with the *Cumberland Sunday Times.*

The tombstone notes that the general was "killed" rather than died. The Frostburg Museum has some recollections from Arthur Irwin who is the son in A.J. Irwin and Son. The Irwin family operated a monument business on Main Street in Frostburg for many decades.

The interviewer wrote, "About the time of the Civil War, an officer on his way back from Washington DC with his mustering out pay was murdered and buried on Meadow Mountain. Sometime later, Red's father made a copy of the inscription made on a wooden grave marker. He then made a stone monument for the grave which can be seen as you ride by on Route 40."

A 1992 article in the *Cumberland Times-News* talked to Donald Workman, who was a retired history teacher in Allegany County. He had researched the story of Gen. Scofield, talking to "old timers." One of the stories he was told was that Scofield was killed in a buggy accident.

"That seems logical," Workman told the newspaper. "It could be that the man was wearing remnants of a Civil War uniform and carried a card or papers identifying him as Scofield."

While this makes sense, no mention of a murder or a death of a veteran or a general is made when searching through the area newspapers in 1894.

The man buried in the grave is not any known General Scofield. Research through Civil War veteran databases and pension records shows only two Civil War generals with the last name of Scofield.

The better known of the two is General John Schofield who died in Florida in 1906 and is buried in Arlington National Cemetery. He led Union troops in Missouri, Tennessee, Georgia and North Carolina during the Civil War. After the war, he served as U.S. Secretary of War under President Andrew Johnson.

Hiram Scofield died in Iowa in 1906 and is buried there. He served throughout the South during the war and commanded the Eighth Louisiana Regiment Colored Troops while he was a colonel.

Thinking that General Scofield might have attained the rank of general after the Civil War, I looked through various databases. In searching through the National Park Service's database of Civil War veterans, you can find 444 men who served with the last name of Scofield. I checked Union pension records for Scofields in Maryland and Pennsylvania. Nine names came up Six had death dates listed that weren't in 1894. The other three had no death dates listed. Their names were Henry, Herman W., and Hunter J. However, no reference can be found that any of them were generals.

Marie Lancaster also spent much of her last years until her death in 2001 trying to figure out who General Scofield was.

"We never really could get to the bottom of anything," said her son, Robert.

He said his mother always felt a connection to the site because her grandfather was a Civil War veteran who was forgotten in a way.

When William Michael Loar returned home from fighting in the war for its entirety, he walked up a lane to a house and asked the two women there if he could have a bite to eat. The women were gracious and invited the war veteran in for supper.

As Loar sat down to eat at the kitchen table, he said to the older of the two women, "Mother, don't you know me?"

Neither Loar's wife or mother had recognized him after being gone for four years.

Loar was lucky. He was able to reunite with his family. The unknown veteran's family probably wondered what had happened to their brother/father/husband/son for the rest of their lives, never knowing he was buried beneath the ground and the wrong name on Meadow Mountain.

LEGENDS AND FOLKLORE

Is There Forgotten Silver in Garrett County?

In the early 1800s, George Layman went out hunting one day in what is now Northern Garrett County. He walked for quite some time searching for game that seemed to have abandoned the area. At some point, he realized that not much around him was looking familiar. He was lost.

Back then, you couldn't whip out a smartphone and call up a map or call for help. You couldn't even walk and hope to reach a paved road. There just weren't many roads around.

So Layman started heading in the direction he thought was home, but it was still quite a hike.

"Tired and thirsty, he came at last to a free-flowing mountain spring. After quenching his thirst and while resting beside the spring, he noticed an outcropping of rock that was like nothing he had ever seen before," an article by Ross C. Durst in *Tableland Trails* noted.

The rock had a metallic sheen to it, and when he broke off a piece, it was heavier than he expected. He shoved it into his pocket and started walking again.

He made it back home and forgot all about the curious rock that he had found. He set it on a shelf and allow neighbors to be surprised by its appearance.

One friend was more than surprised, though. He convinced Layman to have the rock assayed. Layman agreed, and it turned out that there was silver in the rock. It was extracted and minted into coins that would be worth around $250 today.

"Daniel Layman, son of George and the writer's uncle, carried one of these silver half-dollars as a pocket-piece during most of his life," Durst noted.

Knowing that his rock had been only a piece of a much larger stone, Layman tried to find the original rock once again.

"The lapse of time had erased most of the details and the face of nature had changed," Durst wrote. "Nature seems to have exposed her secret for a moment then dropped the curtain. A century later, her secret is still undisclosed."

After years of unsuccessfully searching for the outcropping on his own, Layman told his family of the only clues that he could remember. One was that the stream next to the rock had been flowing east and that he believed the spring had been on the west side of Meadow Mountain.

Durst said these clues actually narrowed the search because relatively few of the springs on the west side of the mountain flowed east. However, no amount of searching has ever yielded a silver lode.

"If the lode is ever discovered it will probably be entirely accidental just as was the original discovery," Durst wrote.

The story of Layman's lost silver vein is believed to have attracted a pair of prospectors from Arizona who came into northern Garrett County searching for silver.

When they discovered silver on the farm of Hiram Duckworth, they decided to form a mining company for a mine they named the Silver Belle and issue stock to raise capital to extract the silver. Bankers in Lonaconing invested heavily in the mine and Georges Creek coal miners were hired to mine the silver.

The problem was when they went to work, they found no

paying ore.

The mine eventually failed, and the finger pointing began, but it seems that the original miners had used the story of Layman's lost mine as a stock-selling scheme.

While there have been small deposits of gold found in Maryland (mainly in Central Maryland), no paying silver deposits have ever been found. However, there is a story of a lost silver mine in Carroll County near the town of Silver Run.

Cursed Land in Garrett County

I n Garrett County, somewhere around Swallow Falls or McHenry, there is a plot of land that may be "cursed".

Early in the 19th century, Joseph Friend, who was a son-in-law of the Western Maryland frontiersman Meshack Browning, built a home midway between Sang Run and Oakland. In 1823, Friend had married Rachael Browing, who was the second of 11 children born to Meshack Browning and his first wife, Mary McMullen.

Meshach Browning has been called Maryland's most famous frontier hunter. He also explored much of Western Maryland. He remains well known today because of his memoir *Forty-Four Years of the Life of a Hunter*, which was first published in 1859.

Browning's father, Joshua, was an English soldier who survived Braddock's massacre in 1755. He deserted the army and settled in Western Maryland to make his way as a woodsman.

Meshach Browning learned these skills growing up. He was drafted into the military as a sergeant and served for a short time in the War of 1812. After the war, he returned home to hunt and explore. Browning estimated in his book that during his lifetime he killed "from 1800 to 2000 deer, from 300 to 400 bears, and about 50 panthers and catamounts, with scores of wolves and wildcats."

Friend's home, in what would eventually become Garrett County, was his dream home for his family until it burned down killing two of Friend's sons.

The Evening Times lists the two children who died as John, 8, and Freeman, 10. However, a family tree compiled by a branch of the family indicates that Joseph Friend and Rachael Browning had 10 children, but only two of them died in the same year. Mahlon and John both died in 1839. These two boys were also two years apart for a portion of the year while Freeman and John were nine years apart.

Rachael Browning Friend

"Mr. Friend, thinking that the occurrence was one of those awful accidents that sometimes happens, rebuilt, but when his house burned down the second time in the same mysterious way that it did the first, he thought it was very strange and refused to rebuild and moved elsewhere," the newspaper reported.

Friend sold the property to a man whose last name was Bray. He knew about the mysterious fires that had burned down two homes. Undeterred, Bray built his home on the old foundation only to have it burn down a short time later.

Bray wasn't ready to give up. "Mr. Bray, like Mr. Friend, concluded that he would not rebuild on the old site or foundation, so he changed the location and had his new house erected near the old foundation," *The Evening Times* reported.

In 1899, Bray's second home burned down. The fire from

the house also jumped to the large barn that stood a few yards away from the house.

"Mr. Bray, like the former owner, also concludes that the spot is doomed, and will not again replace the buildings. He is terribly worried about the matter as all he has is wrapped up in his little farm," the newspaper reported.

Rachael Friend died in 1869 in Deer Park and Joseph died in 1894 in Sang Run.

The unknown plot of cursed land remains waiting for the next home to be built upon it.

LIFE IN GARRETT COUNTY

A Ride Through The Western Maryland Countryside

O n a lovely June day in 1856, 10 men left Baltimore on the Baltimore and Ohio Railroad to travel its length and see the country. A special train consisting of an engine, dining car, two cars with reading rooms and writing rooms, and a passenger car carried them on comfort on their journey. One of the men, Brantz Mayer, wrote about the trip and *Harper's Weekly* published it in April 1857.

The iconic Harper's Weekly began in 1857 as "a journal of civilization." It became famous for its coverage of the Civil War and sketches of the events. This early version ceased publication 1916, although several revivals have been attempted over the years.

Mayer noted that it was only recently that people could enjoy their trips into the mountains. "It has only been of late that bolder minds have ventured to restore romance to travel by scaling the Alleghanies with steam-engines, and making a jaunt through our upland dells and forests as great a delight as it was to those who first penetrated our wilderness," he wrote.

It was raining when the group reached Cumberland at around 4 p.m. Mayer wrote, we "were soon relieved from anxiety as to accommodations by our generous friends in this charming city. We should do violence to their feelings if we spoke publicly of what is habitual with them and characteristic of the country; but we should equally violate ours if we avoided the expression of gratitude for a pleasant season in Cumberland, spent in the midst of unostentatious people and 'old Maryland hospitality.'"

One of the engravings from the *Harper's Weekly* article showing Cranberry Grade.

The following morning the group boarded a special train owned by the Eckhart Mining Company to get a tour of the county's coal region. Mayer described the Narrows as "splendid gap, which extends for more than a mile, five hundred feet wide, with precipitous walls of near nine hundred!"

Mayer wrote that the Eckhart Mining Company must be one of the prosperous businesses in the district "owning a railway, several villages, ten thousand acres of coal land, immense quantities of timber and farming country, and employing about six hundred workmen."

Mayer had been in a coal mine previously, so he did not take the tour of the pit with the other men in the group. Instead, he sat on the hillside admiring the panorama view.

They then took a carriage ride further up the mountain

and saw "a vestige of Braddock's Road, which the patriotic owner has fenced in, for fifteen or twenty yards, as a post-and-rail monument to the defeated General?"

They also passed through Frostburg "a fresh mountain village, flourishing under the impetus of an increasing neighborhood."

Then it was on to Mount Savage with its mix of industry and "cultivated society."

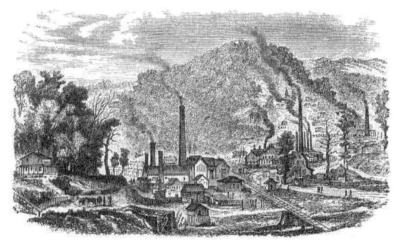

One of the engravings from the *Harper's Weekly* article showing Mount Savage Iron Works.

They finally returned to Eckhart and rode the Eckhart Mines train back to Cumberland.

"I know few inland towns more charmingly situated than Cumberland, on the slope of a superb amphitheatre, with its background of mountains, approached through vistas of forest-covered spurs," Mayer wrote.

He noted that most traces of the old historic Fort Cumberland had vanished and was replaced with new growth. They did walk the hill where the fort had been located walking around a "Gothic Church, which occupies the site of the fort, and 'whose *canons'* as a joker said, 'have displaced the *cannons* of the fort.'" He noted that a depression in the ground marked the site of the old well that had served the fort.

One of the engravings from the *Harper's Weekly* article showing the Narrows in Allegany County.

On Greene Street, the group was shown two houses that were supposedly built by General Braddock. They were made of heavy timbers with iron bands and rivets on the side. Although they were homes in 1856, originally they were supposed to have been a jail and a court.

Late in the day, the group boarded the B&O Special and headed south, skirting along the Potomac River to New Creek in Virginia (modern-day Keyser, W.Va.).

From there, the group left the Savage Valley and entered Crabtree Gorge alongside the Allegheny Mountains. When they reached a few miles above Frankville, the men looked back and caught a glimpse of "one of the grandest views in the mountains. The gloomy masses of Savage Mountain tower on the right, fold upon fold, and the eastern slopes of Meadow Mountain, with its spurs, on the left; while between them the Savage River winds away for miles and miles in a silvery trail till it is lost in the distance," Mayer wrote.

One of the engravings from the *Harper's Weekly* article showing Eckhart Mines in Allegany County.

They passed from Piedmont to Altamont ascending the mountain. At Altamont, they began a slight descent into the Glades. Mayer found the Glades beautiful mountain meadows. "It is rich in all the natural grasses that delight a herdsman, relieved by islands of white-oak interspersed with alder; it is full of copious streams, kept full and fresh by the clouds that condense round the summits; its waters are alive with trout, and waste themselves in deep cascades and falls after furnishing pools for the fish; it pastures innumerable herds of sheep, whose tenderness and flavor rival that of the deer which abound in the woods; wild turkeys and pheasants hide among its oaks, beeches, walnuts, and magnolias; the sugar maple supplies it with a tropical luxury in abundance; the woods are vocal with larks, thrushes, and mocking-birds; and in the flowering season nothing is gayer than the meadows with their showy flowers," he wrote.

The train then pulled into Oakland, seven years old, although not yet incorporated. Mayer found it "as a sort of nestling-place for folks who are willing to be satisfied by being cool, quiet, and natural during summer."

Although it was summer, the night was cold, and Mayer said the men "were not reluctant to ensconce ourselves beneath blankets."

Mayer foresaw a day when the area would be popular with people seeking to improve their health or find nature.

"There are numbers of reasonable people who must be eager to quit the beaten paths, and escape to spots where they will not be stifled by society: and these glades and mountain streams, with their constant coolness and verdure, are precisely the places for them," Mayer wrote.

He suggested that a cook who was inventive with venison and trout could make his fortune in Oakland and attract a following.

The next morning, he noted how the mists hung low to the ground well after sunrise, and the air was so cold that the men wore their overcoats.

They boarded their train once again and headed west toward the Ohio River.

Let It Snow! Oh, No!

T he call came in that Thomas J. Johnson required an ambulance. He was seriously ill and needed to get to the hospital. Normally, it wouldn't be a problem, but in early 1958, getting anywhere in Garrett County was, to say the least, difficult.

The ambulance attempted to reach him, but it couldn't get through to Johnson's Herrington Manor home. Help came in the form of bulldozers and snowplows that struggled to carve a path through drifting snow as high as 15 feet. It took six hours for the plows to reach the 67-year-old Johnson and rush him to Garrett Memorial Hospital.

During another incident that winter, Trooper First Class Robert Henline walked three miles through deep snow that vehicles couldn't get through to deliver medicine to a desperate family near Gorman.

Other incidents occurred, some serious and some just major inconveniences, but there were a lot of them. In seven weeks in 1958, nearly 112 inches of snow fell on the county, beating out the previously severe winter of 1936. No other winter in the 20th century to that point even came close.

The *Cumberland Sunday Times* reported that the bad weather "practically isolated most of the county despite heroic efforts of State Roads and county roads crews, National Guardsmen and other volunteers."

Although the first snows of the new year had fallen mid-January, the first big storm came at the end of the month. Ten inches of snow fell on January 24 followed by three more inches two days later. "For a short time on Friday afternoon there was snow, sleet and ice falling at the same time," *The Republican* reported. A dense fog also slowed things down.

The heavy snows led to the rare occurrence of closing Garrett County schools in the county for three days at the beginning of February.

"It was the first time in several years that there had been the loss of even one day of school," *The Republican* noted.

School Superintendent Willard Hawkins said he "was afraid to put the buses on the roads because of poor visibility and icy conditions." *The Republican* reported that Hawkins had intended to resume school on the third day until he found out that many children and teachers were still snowbound.

A week later nearly 10 inches of snow fell on three consecutive days. Pleasant Valley, Kempton, North Glade, Sanders Lane, and Herrington Manor were the worst hit, reporting snow drifts of 15 feet or more. With visibility near zero, the Maryland State Police issued an emergency travel only order.

The blizzard left about 40 percent of the county roads impassable for two days, according to Paul DeWitt, assistant county engineer. Garrett County had 140 men working 45 snow plows around the clock to try and open and clear the 740 miles of county roads.

State road crews were running 20 snow plows and a giant snowblower over the 158 miles of state roads in the county. The only state road that was impassable was Route 495 between Bittinger and Grantsville.

With so much snow on the ground, the snow plows were only able to push it so far off the road before running into previous piles of snow that had been pushed off the road. "By that time there was no place to push it and consequently many of the highways drifted completely over," *The Republican* reported.

A picture of how high the snow can pile up in Garrett County during the winter. Photo courtesy of the Garrett County Historical Society.

In Oakland, snow and vehicles competed for space and the snow often won. "Parking space was at a premium and many of those who found places at the edges of the drifts found themselves unable to move when they returned to their cars," *The Republican* noted.

All of the snow busted the county's budget that year with rented equipment costing $1,000 a day and snow removal equipment using 2,000 gallons of gasoline a day.

Although the snow totals blew away previous snowfall

records in the county, at least the temperature records still stood. In 1958, the temperature fell to -17 degrees, but the 1912 record was -40 degrees.

Wolf Hunting in Garrett County

S Am Beachy waited for nightfall when the only light to see by came from the moon. He motioned for his dog Brandy to follow him and then the two of them started down toward the Casselman River.

Sensing the seriousness of the mission, Brandy kept silent but alert. Beachy was likewise alert and quiet.

Soon, he began hearing howling from among the alder brush along the river's edge. The timber wolves had arrived.

"The large grey timber wolves abounded throughout the county; and in some localities they kept up such a hideous howling at night that folks got out of bed, took a tin horn and blew a loud blast to scare the prowlers away," according to an article in the *Journal of the Alleghenies*.

Wolves have been hunted for nearly 13,000 years for sport, their skins and to protect livestock. It's uncertain as to whether Beachy was hunting wolves for sport or to reduce the danger to area livestock.

The danger from wolves, in terms of livestock loss, was so great in the 19th century that bounties were often offered for wolf hides. A wolf hide could fetch a bounty of $15 to $30 in the late 1800s, depending on its size. This would be an estimated $700 to $1,400 today.

A hunter earned this money, too. Wolves were difficult to catch in a steel trap. "They showed almost human shrewdness in avoiding a baited trap. A wolf might slink up within sight of a dead carcass and stop at a safe distance. Then he would slip away and stay for perhaps a week, only to return again. If on his second visit he found nothing changed in the least, he crept up to the carcass for a meal," according to the *Journal of the Alleghenies.*

Wolves used to be numerous enough in Garrett County to be hunted. Photo courtesy of Wikimedia Commons.

Beachy waited behind a haystack near the old bridge crossing the river. The planks from the bridge had been removed leaving only the underlying sleepers.

Brandy crept across the bridge on the sleepers and began to follow a scent on the other side. Before too long, a pack of wolves was chasing after Brandy. The dog headed back across the bridge with the wolves in hot pursuit.

"One of the wolves in the lead chasing the dog was about half the distance across the sleeper when Uncle Sam let drive at him broadside, and the wolf fell into the river," according to the *Journal of the Alleghenies.*

Beachy couldn't see the wolf's body in the dark, so he went to bed and came back in the morning to search for the wolf. He was still unable to find it. Cursing his lost bounty,

Beachy went to work.

Months later, Holmes Wiley caught a wolf that was half starved. He saw that it had been wounded around its kidneys. After some discussion, it was decided that this was the wolf that Beachy had shot. It must have survived the injury, but apparently, the wound impaired the wolf's ability to hunt.

In the late 1870s, 100,000 wolves were killed annually in the United States. In Maryland, gray wolves had virtually disappeared by the turn of the 20th century, according to the Maryland Department of Natural Resources.

"Some species disappeared from Maryland, and a few of these even became extinct rangewide. Elk, bison, wolves, and cougars have disappeared from the state, while the carrier passenger pigeon and Carolina parakeet are now extinct," according to the Maryland Department of Natural Resources website.

A New County from Allegany and Garrett

G arrett wasn't even a decade old when word started spreading that there was a move afoot to slice out a western portion of Allegany County and eastern portion of Garrett County to form yet another new county in Western Maryland.

"For a number of years past a few individuals living in Frostburg and vicinity have been agitating the question of carving a new county our of parts of Allegany and Garrett counties—for what purpose has never been definitely states, unless it is to create more offices. It certainly cannot be said the Georges Creek region has not a full share of offices in Allegany county at this time," the *Alleganian and Times* reported in 1878.

It had reached the point that freshman legislator Joseph Benson Oder, a Democrat on the Allegany County delegation in the House of Delegates submitted a bill that many believed, if passed, would form a new county.

Garrett County had been formed in 1872 from the westernmost end of Allegany County, and the newspaper noted, "Allegany has been divided, and we venture to say if the people of Garrett had the privilege of voting again on the subject they would gladly return to their former allegiance."

The *Alleganian and Times* clearly came down on the side that it was a bad idea. The newspaper article pointed out that Allegany County had very little debt at the time and that all of the necessary public buildings had been built and paid for at a great cost to the taxpayers, some of whom would be living in the new county. Forming a new county not only meant that new public buildings would need to be constructed in a new county seat (which most likely would have Frostburg), but residents of the new county would have to pay their pro rata share of the existing Allegany County debt.

Not even the potential residents of the new county were pleased with what was happening.

A Frostburg resident wrote to *The Mining Journal* criticized the decision saying, in part, "Ye Frostburg lunatics, if you are submerged, ye Lonaconing lunatics, must go down with the 'All for truth.'"

The *Alleganian and Times* went so far as to suggest that the new county move wasn't so much something to benefit the citizens, but a way to create more government jobs "for the especial benefit of men too lazy or too ignorant to make a decent living for themselves?"

Oder, who was the former editor of *The Mining Journal*, finally wrote to the *Alleganian and Times* to try and explain his bill.

"Hence, I am amazed that both the measure alleged and myself have been so grossly misunderstood by an intelligent community," Oder wrote.

He said the bill was actually a Garrett County bill proposed by the Garrett County delegation, not Oder.

"It provides for the passage of certain local laws of Allegany county in force at the time of division, but never reenacted for Garrett county," Oder wrote. "In framing the title of the present bill it was necessary to quote the title of the act of 1872, which provided for the 'formation of a new county,' etc. That is all." He added that the bill was "harmless."

Harmless or not, it went through three readings and was

never introduced in the House of Delegates, which may have been due in part from the public outcry.

Oder served only one term in the Maryland House of Delegates from 1878 to 1880. He was a native Virginian, who had fought in the Civil War as a Confederate soldier and was present at the battles of Cold Harbor, Malvern Hill, Chancellorsville, Winchester, and Gettysburg. According to J. Thomas Scharf's *History of Western Maryland.*

The fellow members of the Allegany County delegation during Oder's term were William Brace, Jr. (R), Patrick Carroll (D), and William McMahon McKaig (D).

Garrett County's First Phone Call

Hen Alexander Graham Bell said, "Mr. Watson, Come here, I want to see you" into an early version of the telephone, it wouldn't be heard in Garrett County until 1900.

William A. Smith of Hoyes built the first telephone line in the county between the general stores in Sang Run and Hoyes. This allowed callers to speak with one another, but only in those two locations.

"This is considered remarkable when one realizes Bell secured his Patent in 1876, the A. T. & T. company was formed in 1884 and 16 years later when the Bell had hardly gotten out of New Haven, Connecticut, we find a telephone line constructed and operating so far away from the field of the then telephone activity," W. Russell Pancake, engineer assistant with the C & P Telephone Company told the Oakland Rotary Club in 1952.

Smith quickly realized the popularity of the telephone as he watched people flock to the store to use it. He also realized its time-saving qualities and the good that it could bring in connecting communities. He joined with M. Mattingly of Hoyes, Joseph H. McCrobie of Oakland, C. V. Guard of Friendsville, William Miller of Accident, and J. N. Durst of New Germany to form the Garrett County Telephone Company.

They placed their first switchboard in the A. D. Naylor store where Paul Naylor was one of the first operators. The benefit of having a switchboard was that it allowed any subscriber on the system to be connected to any other subscriber unlike the original line that only allowed the subscribers on either end of the line to communicate.

The company began stringing phone lines across the county, but also across the county and state lines to connect Garrett County with the world. The Garrett County Telephone Company went into Lonaconing in Allegany County, and Mount Storm, Elk Garden, Davis, Thomas, Terra Alta, and Cranesville in West Virginia.

One of the places in the county that the Garrett County Telephone Company didn't reach was Kitzmiller, but the residents there got their phone service in 1906. A phone company based across the Potomac River in Blaine, W.Va., was established in 1906. R. A. Smith Coal and Coke Company in Blaine was the first subscriber on the system, but on the Maryland side, three subscribers were connected in 1906. These were the Browning residence, the First National Bank, and the Blaine Mercantile Company, all in Kitzmiller.

The C & P Telephone Company started in Oakland on July 31, 1906. The company took over the phone service in Oakland including the 95 subscribers on the Garrett County Telephone Company. The first C & P switchboard was a one-position magneto switch that was installed at 58 Second Street over the Harned Drug Store.

Phones on a magneto switch are phones initially required the caller to use a hand crank to create a charge that signaled other phones on the party line that it was in use and also the operator at the local exchange.

Dr. Henry McComas, who had an office in the same building as C & P, was the first subscriber to the system outside of the subscribers that C & P took over from Garrett County Telephone Company.

C & P also took over the telephone company in Blaine and its 34 subscribers in 1920. When the takeover was made, the subscribers were also switched over to rotary dial telephones, although the phone system did not allow for direct dialing.

"If you would ask the average individual when dial telephones came into use, you would probably get the answer of the 1920's, for that is when they became general over the United States," Pancake said. "Yet machine switching, as we call it, is as old as the telephone itself."

The rotary dial telephones were based on the Strowger Switch invented in 1889, and as Pancake noted, their use in telephones started replacing magneto phones in a large scale beginning in the 1920's.

Unable to keep up with the changes and maintenance required for a telephone company and its shrinking subscriber base, the Garrett County Telephone Company closed in 1922. The remaining 42 subscribers were transferred to C & P.

From then one, C & P was the telephone company that serviced Garrett County and instituted improvements in telephone communications.

Boy Held Prisoner in Chains

T he young boy cried until he had no more tears. Not that it mattered no one was around to hear him. His father was in the coal mine in Kitzmiller working, and his mother was in the house doing chores. His brothers and sisters were either working, in the house, or playing somewhere else.

Tommy Wilson pulled at the iron collar clamped around his neck. He'd been pulling and wiggling it for a couple hours, hoping that it would open. He "at times gave up in despair and from exhaustion, only to renew his efforts later," according to the *Baltimore News*. It hadn't. It was screwing around his neck snugly. He only managed to make the skin on his neck raw.

He pulled at the end of the heavy chain that was fastened to the collar. There was no seam or weakness that he could find there.

So he traced the end of the chain back to where his father had fastened it to the ground. When he pulled hard that end wiggled. It was loose, so he worked it back and forth for long minutes until the ground around the spike widened and the spike that held the chain attached to the ground popped free.

Tommy ran to a neighbor's house. "Still fearing that he might be betrayed and sent back to captivity once more, he sought refuge under the building hoping he would not be discovered," the *Baltimore News* reported.

He lay there in the dirt and darkness of the crawlspace under the house. He was too afraid to worry about eating, and he was exhausted from his struggles against the chain.

He was found several hours later after his family had discovered him missing.

The following day he was once again chained to the ground, although his father made sure the anchor was secure this time. This was Tommy's punishment for venturing out into the woods to play when he was told not to by his parents.

While Tommy suffered his miserable situation, the neighbors hadn't forgotten the sight of the boy with the chain around his neck. They called the authorities, and a deputy made the trip to the Wilson home in Kitzmiller. The deputy found Tommy chained by the neck and bound to his father's house in Kitzmiller, Garrett county, with heavy irons bearing the chain down to make his captivity secure," according to the newspaper.

Tommy was taken from the home on the charge "of being a minor without proper care," although his nine siblings were still left in the care of their parents. After given a check-up, he was put aboard a train to Baltimore where he was taken under the care of Henry Watson Children's Aid Society. While there, he was expected to "undergo treatment to restore him to good physical condition before a final disposition of his case is made."

When the hearing was held in Oakland, Tommy's father attended, but he appeared indifferent, according to the newspaper.

"Do what you please with him, the miner is said to have told the magistrate," the *Baltimore News* reported.

Tommy's mother did not appear at the hearing.

The outcome of the hearing is not known. Tommy may have been placed in foster care and returned to his family at some future time.

An *Ancestry.com* search shows that the most-likely Tommy Wilson in this story was born in1903 to Daniel and

Nellie Wilson. There are some problems with this being the Tommy Wilson in the story, though. Although the birth year would fit and Daniel Wilson a coal miner, these Wilsons lived in Westernport in 1910. However, Daniel had lived in Garrett County in the past, and the family did move sometime after 1910 back to Garrett County in the vicinity of Kitzmiller. The other discrepancy is that this Wilson family did not have 10 children. One possible explanation is that the older children did not live in the home and the Wilsons had another child or two after the census was taken.

If this is the Tommy Wilson in the story, then the poor lived a short, tragic life. In 1917, 14-year-old Payne Culp shot and killed Tommy who was also 14 at the time. It happened at the Red Oak School on March 16. Tommy was apparently a member of a gang at the school that was bullying Culp, and Culp took matters into his own hands and shot Tommy, according to the *Cumberland Evening Times.*

Soldiers and Their Music

War can certainly be a time of danger, but there are other times when soldiers are in camp stateside or behind the lines when they can relax.

Camp Meade near Laurel was named for Maj. Gen. George Meade. It became an active army installation in 1917. During World War I, more than 400,000 soldiers passed through the camp to be trained for the war. It was the training site for three infantry divisions, three training battalions, and one depot brigade.

During the course of the war, 704 Garrett Countians served in the military, and most of them were sent to Camp Meade for training. The Garrett County boys in Camp Meade in October 1917 were part of a company of 250 men from Garrett and Allegany counties and Baltimore City. The traveling agent with the B&O Railroad who had charge of the Garrett County recruits when they were taken to Camp Meade, said of them, "The boys from Garrett county were the finest bunch I have so far taken to any camp."

Once at camp, their training went well. "We arrived safely in camp and most everyone is well and getting along fine with our drills, considering the time we have been here," six of the recruits – Henry Byrn Hamill, Earl W. Alexander, Harry M. Setzer, Paul R. Liston, Robert R. Glotfelty, John W. Livengood – wrote in a letter to *The Republican*.

They were healthy and happy. *The Republican* described them as "the finest specimens of young manhood in the country."

They were bored, though.

The six recruits, who were representing all of the Garrett County recruits, asked if a subscription fund could be started to buy them a Victrola "as the time when off duty would pass much faster if we had a Victrola to cheer up the boys from 'Old Garrett,' and serve to keep them from getting blue," the letter read.

Although today, Victrola has become a generic term for old phonographs, back then a Victrola was a brand of phonographs with an internal horn that was manufactured by the Victor Talking Machine Company. They are not the older versions of phonographs that Victor used in its logo. This model had an external horn, and a dog sat in front of the horn to hear his master's voice.

True Victrolas were first marketed in 1906 and quickly gained popularity. That popularity helped bring down the price to roughly $100 ($1,870 today) depending on where it was purchased.

The Republican staff jumped into action starting the sub-scription fund not only for a Victrola but also records that could be played on it. Not waiting for the next issue, staff began notifying people in town about the request.

Within an hour after the subscription efforts began, $46.50 in donations had come into the newsroom from 41 donors. E. H. Sincell pledged the most ($5) and some people pledged as little as 25 cents.

One minister gladly donated a dollar to the fund, telling the editor, "Never do you start anything for the boys again unless I am in on the ground floor. If this is insufficient for the purpose or if you want to raise another fund for anything else come to me."

The citizens of Friendsville took up a collection and raised $11 from 11 donors. The Girls Club of Gormania raised another $5 and mailed it to the newspaper office.

After a week, $83 had been raised from 74 donors. Within two weeks the $100 goal had been surpassed, and the boys from Garrett County had an enjoyable way to pass the time by the end of October.

This is the model Victrola that the citizens of Garrett County raised funds to buy for WWI soldiers. Photo courtesy of Wikimedia Commons.

Was It Against the Law to Marry in Oakland?

"**A**rrest him when he gets to Oakland and hold the girl until we get there."

It was an all-too-familiar call that the Clerk of the Circuit Court and Garrett County Sheriff used to receive from someone trying to prevent a marriage from taking place in Oakland.

"There is no law against a man thinking that he would like to get married, and even going so far as to get the consent of his 'one and only' and bringing her to Oakland for that purpose, but judging from the number of letters and telephone calls received at the office of the Clerk of the Circuit Court and by the Sheriff of Garrett county, practically everyone appears to think so," *The Republican* reported in 1930 just before Valentine's Day.

Maryland was a popular location for couples seeking to elope because there was no waiting period involved. Many of the calls and letters came from people in either West Virginia or Pennsylvania who were trying to stop a wedding of couples from those states.

The county clerk's office alone received four to five letters a day about issuing a marriage license, and that didn't include the phone calls. Some people were asking for information, but some sought way too much information. For instance, one letter writer might ask for six weeks' worth of marriage data, including the name of the parties marrying, their places of residence, their ages, their occupations, and the name of the minister who married them. This could tie up the clerk's office for a day to gather it.

"Other letters come in asking that a license be not issued to Miss Take and Mr. Nogood for various reasons," according to *The Republican.*

These were the ones that raised concern because the county clerk didn't want to issue a license to a couple that was ineligible for one for some hidden reason. However, it was also possible that the caller was joking, a rival stalling for time, or someone with a grudge against either the bride or the groom.

"The only thing we can do in cases like these is to question the applicant more closely than usual, and tell him the consequences of perjuring himself," said A. G. Ross, deputy clerk of the court.

With the applicants under oath, it gave their answers to the clerk's questions more weight than a caller who was not under any obligation to tell the truth.

"If the applicant, under affidavit, says he is 21 years of age, and the girl eighteen years of age, and other questions are satisfactorily answered, there is no reason why a license should not be issued," Ross said.

It didn't stop people from trying to halt a wedding, though.

"But the letters and telephone messages continue to come and probably will continue until Oakland ceases to become the mecca for prospective husbands and wives," *The Republican* noted.

Wear It Out and Use It Again

D uring the Great Depression, money was tight for many organizations as well as individuals. President Franklin D. Roosevelt's alphabet agencies provided a lot of work for unemployed people as well as improving the quality of life for residents where the work was done.

The Maryland Library Commission sponsored a program that brought the Works Progress Administration (WPA) to Maryland communities to renovate and restore damaged books in western Maryland public libraries.

"Because of these projects several thousand dollars have been saved by school boards and libraries to use for the purchase of new books," *The Republican* reported in 1938.

Western Maryland had six WPA groups working in Oakland, Westernport, Lonaconing, and Cumberland. The groups worked out of space donated by county school boards and public libraries. A year into the program, which began on February 16, 1937, 3,451 books had been restored for Garrett County libraries and schools. Over the 18 months, the program would run, the goal was to restore 5,250 books. More than 15,000 books were expected to be restored in Allegany County, which had started its program a year before Garrett County.

"The workers have not only been provided employment, but they are learning a useful occupation to pursue when WPA library projects are over," the newspaper reported.

When a book was no longer considered usable, it was sent to a WPA mending unit. The books were then sorted.

Some were beyond repair but were saved to use pages to replace damaged pages in other books of the same title. This was useful for school textbooks where there were multiple copies of the same book.

Each book was then cleaned.

"The workers examine the book for missing pages, remove pencil marks and wash each page. They mend each torn page and neatly 'tip in' the missing pages taken from discarded books. If these missing pages cannot be found, from discarded books, a type written copy of the page is made and inserted," *The Republican* reported.

Next, the worn-out dust jacket was removed and the book placed in a clamp. The WPA worker then used a small hand drill or awl to drill small holes along the book spine. High-quality linen threat was then sewn along the spine through the holes to strengthen the book spine.

If the book's hardcover was no longer any good, new binder boards were cut and covered with a waterproof cloth. These were then attached to the book replacing the damaged hardcover.

Finally, the WPA worker used an electric stylus to write the title, author, and library number on the back of each book.

"When a comparison is made of this neatly mended and lettered copy with one ready for renovating the result seems miraculous, Mrs. Cora G. Perry, supervisor of library projects for Allegany and Garrett counties, told a reporter.

The WPA also helped with cataloging books in the schools and libraries, too. "Through their help, 60,000 volumes have been loaned and 4,000 books cataloged in Allegany and Garrett counties," according to *The Republican*.

More Schooling
for County Students

J ust when the students in Garrett County Schools in 1945 were getting spring fever and looking forward to the fun of no school in the summer, they got some bad news.

Students completing the sixth grade were now going to have to complete 12 years of schooling rather than 11 years. To this point, Garrett County Public Schools had been set up with grades one through seven in elementary schools and grades nine through 12 in high school. There was no grade eight.

The decision to add another year had been made by an educational study group in Oakland in May 1945. The plan was adopted by the Garrett County Board of Education. The board of education then began considering restructuring how schools in the county were set up. They considering putting grades seven through 12 in high schools until junior high schools could be built.

"Regardless of where seventh grade pupils are housed next school year, it is planned that they should have the newly developed courses of study in as complete a form as facilities, materials, and personnel will permit," *The Republican* reported.

Initially, it was believed that if the 12-year plan was adopted that there would be no graduates in Garrett County in 1950. The last 11-year students would graduate in 1949 while the first 12-year students wouldn't graduate until 1951. However, there's no record that this happened.

Garrett County was the fifth county in Maryland to adopt a 12-year school plan. The other jurisdictions that had already started sending students to school for 12 years were Baltimore City, Montgomery County, Allegany County and Washington County.

According to *The Glades Star*, Maryland adopted a 12-year plan in 1946, which meant that all counties were required to follow suit and have a 6-3-3 plan, which Garrett County had already started implementing. This means grades one through six were in elementary schools, grades seven through nine were in junior high schools, and grades 10 through 12 were in senior high schools.

Garrett County integrated its changes with those recommended by the state. On March 22, 1946, the county began preparing its principals and teachers for the reorganization, according to the Garrett County Board of Education minutes.

The first class to go through 12 years of education in Garrett County was the Class of 1951. They were also the first class to go through the eighth grade.

Today, Garrett County Public Schools teaches the 3,900 county students for 13 years. Eight elementary schools now teach students kindergarten through grade five. Junior high schools have become middle schools that teach grades six through 8, and high schools teach grades nine through 12.

I Now Pronounce You Husband and Wife

"We are gathered here to join this man this woman together in matrimony. The contract of marriage is a most solemn one and not to be entered into lightly but thoughtfully and seriously and with deep realization of its obligations and responsibility. If anyone can show just cause why they should not be lawfully joined together let him speak now, or else forever hold his peace," Richard L. Davis said on January 2, 1964, as he performed the first civil marriage in Garrett County.

He stood in a room on the second floor of the Garrett County Courthouse, "decorated especially for the occasion and future civil marriages," according to *The Republican*.

A 1963 act passed by the Maryland General Assembly made it legal for clerks of the circuit court to perform civil marriages. The change took effect with the new year, but since New Year's Day was a legal holiday, the first civil marriages in Maryland couldn't happen until January 2. Maryland was the last state in the country to allow civil marriages.

"Do you take this woman, Margaret Ann Durigon, to be your lawfully wedded wife?" Davis asked. He had to couple join hands. "Now repeat after me, I, Bernard Benjamin Bialon, take this woman, Margaret Ann Durigon, for my lawful wife to have and to hold, from this day forward, for better or for worse, for richer, for poorer, in sickness and in health, until death do us part."

Durigon was 20 years old and lived in Keisterville, Pa. She worked as a stripper for a textile mill. Bialon was 21 years old and lived in Uniontown, Pa. He worked as a machinist for the same mill.

The Garrett County Courthouse where the first civil marriages in the county were performed. Photo courtesy of the Albert and Angela Feldstein Collection.

The small ceremony had no witnesses, but none were required for Maryland marriages. It was just Davis and the couple.

"Place the ring on her finger and say, 'With this ring, I thee wed,'" Davis instructed Bialon.

It was almost accidental that Durigon and Bialon became the first couple married in a civil ceremony in Garrett County. According to *The Republican*, another couple had wanted to be the first couple, but they didn't have the $10 cost for the service.

The cost for a civil ceremony at the time was $10 in addition to an application fee of $1 and a $4 marriage license. Durigon's and Bialon's cost $5 since they were county residents.

From the revenue generated by the license and application fees, $2 went to the county government. In turn, the Garrett County Commissioners turned over 85 percent of the amount to the Ruth Enlow Library and 15 percent to the Garrett County Historical Society. The remaining revenues from the fees stayed in the clerk's office.

Of the $10 cost for the civil ceremony, $8 went into the Garrett County general fund, and $2 went to the clerk's office.

"By the power and authority vested in me as clerk of the Circuit court for Garrett County, Maryland, and I now pronounce you man and wife," Davis said, and so history was made and future created.

In the first eight days of 1964, 24 marriage licenses were applied for, and seven of the couple requested civil ceremonies.

Acknowledgments

I wanted to thank all of those people who helped me put the *Secrets of Garrett County* together. The longer I work as a writer, the more I realize that while one person may publish a book, the effort is much richer when others assist.

To that end, I'd like to thank Eleanor Callis, Bob Boal, and Alice Eary with the Garrett County Historical Society. They graciously allowed me to use some of their pictures in this book, and they also were available to answer questions I might have throughout the process. Eleanor, in particular, put the idea in my head to come up with a book specifically for Garrett County. They were always friendly and generous with their time.

I'd also like to thank Don Sincell, editor of *The Republican* newspaper in Oakland. He has been willing to publish my history articles where many of the chapters in this book got their start.

I always owe Al Feldstein a big thanks. Not only has he been a source of photos and information over the years, but he showed me that independent publishing could work. Taking that path certainly changed my life.

Finally, I'd like to thank Grace Eyler for not only another great-looking cover but also being able to create the template for the Secrets series, of which *Secrets of Garrett County* is the first.

I have probably missed someone who I'll remember after this book goes to print. If so, it's not because I didn't appreciate your input, it's because the gerbil wheel in my head is loose and rolling wildly back and forth.

James Rada, Jr.
January 30, 2017

.

About the Author

J ames Rada, Jr. has written many works of historical fiction and non-fiction history. They include the popular books *Saving Shallmar: Christmas Spirit in a Coal Town, Canawlers,* and *Battlefield Angels: The Daughters of Charity Work as Civil War Nurses.*

He lives in Gettysburg, Pa., where he works as a freelance writer. James has received numerous awards from the Maryland-Delaware-DC Press Association, Associated Press, Maryland State Teachers Association, Society of Professional Journalists, and Community Newspapers Holdings, Inc. for his newspaper writing.

If you would like to be kept up to date on new books being published by James or ask him questions, he can be reached by e-mail at *jimrada@yahoo.com.*

To see James' other books or to order copies on-line, go to *www.jamesrada.com.*

PLEASE LEAVE A REVIEW
If you enjoyed this book, please help other readers find it. Reviews help the author get more exposure for his books. Please take a few minutes to review this book at *Amazon.com* or *Goodreads.com*. Thank you, and if you sign up for my mailing list at *jamesrada.com*, you can get FREE ebooks.

Don't Miss These Books By James Rada, Jr.

Battlefield Angels: The Daughters of Charity Work as Civil War Nurses

The Daughters of Charity were the only trained nurses in the country at the start of the Civil War. Their services were so in demand that they were allowed to cross between the North and the South at the beginning of the war. The served on the battlefields, in hospitals, on riverboat hospitals, and in prisoner-of-war camps.

The Last to Fall: The 1922 March, Battles, & Deaths of U.S. Marines at Gettysburg

In 1922, a quarter of the U.S. Marine Corps marched from Quantico, Va., to Gettysburg, Pa., where they conducted historical re-enactments of Pickett's Charge for 100,000 spectators. The Marines also conducted modern versions of the battle with tanks, machine guns, and airplanes. Two Marines were killed on the battlefield during the exercises making them the last military line-of-duty deaths on the Gettysburg Battlefield.

Made in the USA
Middletown, DE
11 June 2021

41819515R00115